From Battle of Britain Airman to POW Escapee

From Battle of Britain Airman to POW Escapee

The Story of Ian Walker RAF

Angela Walker

Pen & Sword
AVIATION

First published in Great Britain in 2017 by
Pen & Sword Aviation
an imprint of
Pen & Sword Books Ltd
47 Church Street
Barnsley
South Yorkshire
S70 2AS

ISBN 978 1 47389 072 5

A CIP catalogue record for this book is available from the British
Library

Typeset in Ehrhardt by
Mac Style Ltd, Bridlington, East Yorkshire
Printed and bound in the UK by CPI Group (UK) Ltd,
Croydon, CRO 4YY

Pen & Sword Books Ltd incorporates the imprints of Pen & Sword
Archaeology, Atlas, Aviation, Battleground, Discovery, Family
History, History, Maritime, Military, Naval, Politics, Railways,
Select, Transport, True Crime, and Fiction, Frontline Books, Leo
Cooper, Praetorian Press, Seaforth Publishing and Wharncliffe.

For a complete list of Pen & Sword titles please contact
PEN & SWORD BOOKS LIMITED
47 Church Street, Barnsley, South Yorkshire, S70 2AS, England
E-mail: enquiries@pen-and-sword.co.uk
Website: www.pen-and-sword.co.uk

For Sachin & Melanie

May our mountains ever be
Freedom's ramparts on the sea

Thomas Bracken

Contents

Chapter 1

The girl with the poppy

What you leave behind is not what is engraved in stone monuments, but what is woven into the lives of others.

Pericles

How little we sometimes know of the stories that surround us: the stories that are never told, the stories we never ask to hear. Yet events behind our family stories silently shape us like the sea inexorably sculpts a rock. Too painful to recollect but impossible to forget, some things are never spoken. Some of my father's experiences as an airman during the Second World War were buried deep within him; so deep that I had no idea he kept them locked away.

The first inkling I had that my father had been to war was when my family went to the Dawn Parade in 1975. I have a black and white photograph from that day of me as a little girl placing a poppy next to a cross for the Unknown Soldier. A few hours before the photo was taken, my mother had woken me in the wee small hours. Intrigued, I climbed into the back seat of dad's Morris Oxford in the dark of night, my father at the wheel wearing his only suit. No one said much as we drove into the city, towards an Anzac Day ceremony that represented more to him than we could possibly imagine. My anticipation began to build as we arrived at the Auckland War Memorial along with the other early risers. Hundreds of cars were arriving at the Domain, their headlights illuminating long slices of darkness.

Before long the veterans began their solemn march past. Peering through the legs of the people who had gathered to remember, I caught a glimpse of dad marching amongst the other war veterans. Some of them were so old it seemed remarkable to me that they could still walk. My father's face was a study in emotions I didn't understand. I barely recognised the man who passed us by. My father the war veteran was someone I didn't know.

After the formalities, the haunting tones of the Last Post still reverberating in the moist dawn air, I played on the steps beside the cenotaph as we waited for dad to re-join us. As the light continued to build in almost perceptible increments, a photographer captured me crouching down to place my poppy among a group of white crosses. It was a moment that would come to symbolise so much more to me in the years ahead.

I overheard my mother talking to the photographer nearby.

'What newspaper are you from?'

'*The New Zealand Herald*,' he said. 'Your little girl might be in the paper tomorrow.'

On the way home I expect dad was even quieter than usual, haunted by memories sparked during the solemn remembrance of his fallen friends. But he was often quiet, and I was only a child, so I can't say that I noticed.

Early the next morning, my sister Robyn and I, who were always up with the birds, dashed down the front stairs, across the dewy lawn in our slippers, eager to see if I had made it into the newspaper. I grabbed the rolled up newspaper from our letterbox and unrolled it as fast as my hands could move. I'd dared to imagine a small photo buried deep in the heart of the newspaper somewhere, but there, right on the front page, was a large photo of me, poppy in hand. I could scarcely believe my eyes.

A candid shot, it had captured the solemnity of Anzac Day juxtaposed by a young child's innocence far removed from the brutality of war.

It's a photo that speaks to me decades later of someone I've always been. A naive youngster who had no way of knowing the reality of war, unknowingly caught in an unbroken string that ties me to my father, to the Second World War, from the past to the present and to the future. The symbolism of dawn and the poppy had been lost on me. I had no idea what my father had been through to earn those medals pinned to his lapel. I would retain that childlike innocence and the idealism of youth, in what I understood about war and my father, well into my adult years.

Growing up, other than the odd trip to the Dawn Parade, there wasn't anything much about my father that said Second World War airman. War did not define him. Planes didn't particularly fascinate him, and he seemed like someone for whom 'Browning' would evoke the poet not the gun. The war and the Air Force were things from his past that he had largely left behind. It wasn't that he never spoke about the war. He quite happily shared bits and pieces about his wartime days from time to time. Unlike many of his peers, he gave the impression of talking openly and freely about some of his wartime experiences, albeit not very often. Most of his stories evoked adventure or highlighted how fortunate he had been. Back then I had no idea that he skipped over the more traumatic events. The way he seemed quite comfortable, occasionally mentioning his wartime days, masked how much he left unsaid.

Besides, as a child I didn't really have much interest in anything to do with war. Sure, dad had some extraordinary tales to tell at dinnertime. Attempting to escape from a POW camp in Nazi Germany – now that was something. But in my young mind, television programmes such as *Hogan's Heroes* and *Dad's Army* had largely informed my mental pictures. I had no idea about the seriousness of it all. I found it surprising when Battle of Britain enthusiasts would turn up on our doorstep seeking dad's autograph. As one of the heroic 'Few', dad was highly respected by those who remembered the bravery and sacrifice of the men who fought in the Battle of Britain. But as a child on the other side of the world, decades on from the war, the true significance of it all was yet to dawn on me.

Unlike many children of Second World War veterans, I wasn't a post-war baby boomer. Dad was nearly 50 when I was born, and by then the world wars had largely receded to the history books. None of the primary school children I grew up with had even heard of 'the war'. Many of their grandfathers were younger than my dad. When I'd tell my school friends in the playground that my father had been in the war, they'd say, 'What war?' I'm yet to meet many others from Generation X whose father fought 'in the war'. I've met plenty of people a couple of decades older than me whose fathers were involved in the Second World War . They look at me doubtfully when I tell them mine was too.

By the time I grew up and left home, I knew the broad sketch of dad's time at war. During the eight and ninth decades of his life, I enjoyed continuing to get to know him even better, adult-to-adult. I had the privilege of accompanying him to the sixtieth and sixty-fifth anniversaries of the Battle of Britain in London. Now that I was no longer a child, he allowed me to see a little of how he was feeling as we visited places he'd been during the war. They were unique and memorable times. What I didn't realise then, was that this was only the very beginning of my understanding of what he had experienced during the war. Since war horrified me and was something I didn't particularly want to focus on, let alone celebrate, I suppose I was guilty of not asking him much about it. Perhaps I was afraid of what I might learn. How would I feel if my gentle father had killed people during the war? I presumed if you were a Second World War air gunner, you were bound to have killed someone. Perhaps it was easier not to know. So I didn't ask; he didn't say. We talked about a great many things over the years – just not that.

Like most of us, dad had a personal collection of papers and treasures he'd acquired over a lifetime. After he died in 2009, we placed his box of keepsakes in a safe place, anticipating a rainy day where there would be time to look over the contents at leisure.

Three years later I finally found the time to delve into his treasure chest. Dusting it off, I didn't have any expectation of what lay inside. I just knew it was high time his precious things were sorted out. Opening it up, I began to sift through the various faded items in the collection. It wasn't long before I realised I'd unearthed something extraordinary. In the box I discovered his diaries from the 1940s, detailing his wartime experiences day-by-day. I hadn't even known they'd existed. There was a recording* of him describing his time during the war, nestled next to letters, newspaper cuttings and POW camp newspapers – treasures that seemed as though they belonged in a museum. I felt rather in awe of the history I was holding in my hands. I opened up a blue diary marked 1940 and began to read. Soon, I found myself taking a tumultuous journey with my father as he circumnavigated the globe during the war. Words he had written decades earlier transported me to another time and place, illuminating a chapter of his life that had never seen the full light of day. Slowly a picture began to build unlike anything I had ever imagined. I spent day after day lost in the early 1940s. In all the stories he had told me about the war, he had never described the dangerous reality of being in a Wellington bomber in the midst of a night bombing raid to Nazi Germany. I was astounded by what I was reading:

---

* Dr Richard Campbell Begg recorded Ian Walker's memories in 1997 for the Liddle Collection at Leeds University and the Second World War Experience Centre, excerpts of which are included in *For Five Shillings A Day*, by Dr Richard Campbell Begg and Dr Peter Liddle.

25 April 1941 – We are going on operations tonight. Our first trip, they call it 'Freshman trip'! Made careful preparations, cleaned the guns. We have all made our wills etc.... Taking 3000lbs of bombs with us... Arrived over the target about half after midnight... Circled round getting shot at all the time... suddenly... hundreds of searchlights and all hell of a barrage broke out all around us. The concussion of shells threw us about. 'Flaming onions' were curling over my turret in all colours of the rainbow...

Many of the stories dad had shared when I was growing up had been about things that he was happy to recall. In his diaries I found details of events that, understandably, he may not have wanted to remember, and others I fear he could never forget, even if he'd tried. I'd had no idea he'd kept so much to himself. Nor had I known he'd left behind this buried treasure. How could I have been so close to my father yet known so little about his time at war? Had I simply not shown enough interest or had he deliberately kept many of his stories to himself? I guessed we were probably both responsible for my ignorance. I was puzzled that he never mentioned his diaries existed. He had left them amongst his personal possessions, presumably realising they would one day be found. Did he not think anyone would be particularly interested? (Quite possibly given how little interest we had shown.) Did he give any thought to the fact that we would find them after he died, deliberately leaving them as a record for his descendants? Or had he forgotten they existed?

My father was gone, but his voice still remained. As I began to piece together his wartime journey, it felt as though he was speaking to me, changing me in ways I couldn't have anticipated. I began to make more sense of the past and find new ways to decode the world today. The more I learned, the more consumed I became with his story. The details I was discovering in his diaries, and the tales of my childhood, needed a real backdrop. I had a burning desire to travel to the other side of the world and retrace his footsteps during the war. I wanted to better understand what had gone into the making of this wise and resilient man who had influenced and inspired me. There were so many unanswered questions. How had the war shaped him into the person who had shaped me decades later? How different had my father been before the war? What had happened to make him so unlike anyone else I've ever met? I had unearthed a story aching to be told. But would I – the naïve girl with the poppy – be the same person at the end of it all? In 1940, and over seventy years later, an illuminating journey had begun.

Chapter 2

'The boy from Koru'

Last, loneliest, loveliest, exquisite, apart,
On us, on us the unswerving season smiles,
Who wonder 'mid our fern why men depart
To seek the Happy Isles!

Rudyard Kipling

In a far-flung corner of the globe, James 'Ian' Bradley Walker – my father – was born into a large family. The year was 1920 – a fateful year for a boy to be born. By the time he turned 20, the world would be at war and his generation would be called upon to fight for freedom. This would be my father's destiny.

Dad's family lived on a farm in Koru, a little-known place in Taranaki, New Zealand – Aotearoa, the land of the long white cloud, a land the Second World War wouldn't quite reach. When he was born, his mother named him after her brother. Lovingly examining her new-born baby, she noticed that he had a double crown on his head, which was believed to signal good luck. She hoped his double crown would bring him more luck than his namesake, her brother Corporal James Flynn Bradley who had been killed in action at Gallipoli during the First World War.

My father had fond memories of growing up on the farm at Koru with his seven brothers and sisters. The Oakura River ran through the farm creating an idyllic natural playground. As a young boy he was drawn to the river gently flowing over smooth pebbles among the green tangle of ferns, playing there almost every day. He and his siblings spent hours playing on the swing bridge that crossed the stream, making their own fun amid the lush outdoors. From almost every vantage point on the farm, the imposing presence of towering Mount Taranaki could be seen and felt, its snow-capped volcanic cone dominating the landscape. It was beside one of the many awaiti, or streams, of melting snow that flowed from the mountain where the Walker family liked to picnic on Sundays. Once the cows were milked and the cream cans were filled and taken to the factory, they would stroll down to the banks of their very own awaiti, carrying baskets loaded with good things to eat. While the grown-ups rested on brightly coloured rugs, the children searched for brown trout and freshwater crayfish in the stream, and jumped over the grey blue stones that had been put there by the mountain when it erupted long ago, before feasting on homemade ice-cream that had been keeping cool in the icy trickling waters.

The sheer beauty of the place, and the quiet peacefulness it exuded, belied its bloody history. On the other side of the river was an abandoned Maori settlement, Te Koru Pa, the great, fortified village of the Nga Mahanga a Tairi iwi. One of the bloodiest series of battles in Taranaki history had taken place here in the early nineteenth century. Even today, visitors to the old Maori fortification sometimes comment on the extraordinary atmosphere of the place. As a young child, my father had no way of knowing the violent history of the land he stood on, or the future war he would himself experience.

Tragically, at only 3 years of age, he took his first walk through the valley of the shadow of death. One summer's day, he wandered off from a family picnic at a rugged Taranaki beach with his younger sister Doris. All alone, they climbed over rocks, happily exploring the myriad of rock pools and their hidden treasures beneath. Lost in the moment they stumbled on until, in one ill-fated step, his 2-year-old sister fell into the water. What happened next would become a nightmarish blur that my father would rather not remember. Near the end of his life, he shared a few details with me quite out of the blue, confessing his horror at seeing his baby sister drowning at the beach. He had been all alone, not even old enough to go to school. He spoke of his helplessness and inability to do anything. I'd known him all this time and felt surprised that he'd never mentioned he had been there when his little sister had drowned. The local Maori people had come out to help, he said, hanging his sister's body over a smouldering fire, willing the smoke to resurrect her.

Perhaps I should have been alerted to the possibility that there were more stories my father had never told me. But I rationalised that this one had clearly been very traumatic. It didn't seem unreasonable that he had kept it to himself for so long. I wondered if he felt as though he should have been able to do something to save his little sister. Had he felt guilty that he had survived when his sister had drowned? My father only had three innocent years of life before someone close to him died. What would an experience such as this do to someone so young? I guessed, given how tightly he had kept the story to himself, it must have had quite an impact. The tragic loss of his baby sister would foreshadow events yet to come in his life. It wouldn't be the only time he would survive while those around him didn't. His mother cried every day for a year following her daughter's passing. Mount Taranaki had cast a very black shadow over Koru Farm.

For the most part though, dad had fond and happy memories of his early years on the farm. Happily skimming stones on the river, he was blissfully unaware that his parents were rapidly losing the battle to make a living out of the farm. The Great Depression had hit New Zealand hard, and when my father was 7, the Walker family had to 'walk off' their farm and look for work elsewhere. My father left his one room school in Koru about the same time as the 1928 Pact of Paris was being signed. The pact was an international agreement in which countries promised not to use war to resolve conflicts. I doubt my father's family paid much attention to the announcement of this pact as they moved to Auckland. Little matter, it would not succeed.

Given the tough economic times, the Walker clan had no alternative but to move in with Grandma. Her Ponsonby villa, along the snug line-up of ticky-tacky houses on Norfolk Street, was a world away from their stand-alone villa encircled by gently undulating farmland, and my father initially found it tough to adapt to his strange, new world.

Koru is the Maori name given to the new unfurling silver fern frond. Best known as the iconic logo on Air New Zealand planes, it symbolizes new life, growth, strength, peace and awakening. My father would need the essence of Koru forever in his heart as he embarked on a new life in the big city and beyond. One day, the boy from Koru was destined to go on one hell of an adventure, on a journey that would circumnavigate the globe. Some of his experiences, he would talk about for years to come. Others would remain coiled inside him as tightly wound as the koru itself.

But all new silver fern fronds eventually unfurl.

* * *

Growing up, I enjoyed hearing dad occasionally regale us with stories from his youth. My mum and sister and I usually did most of the talking around the dinner table. As the only male in the house, dad rarely bothered to try and get a word in. But when he did speak, we'd hang on his every word. It was partly because he didn't usually have much to say, and partly because his stories were from another time and place far beyond our imagination. Like the time he told us he'd left school at 13.

Sitting calmly at the head of the table where he always sat, he was uncharacteristically talkative over lunch that day.

'Did you know,' dad said looking up from his plate, 'when I was a boy at Kowhai Junior High School, I was in the same class as Robert Muldoon.'

Robert Muldoon was the Prime Minster of New Zealand at the time, so he had our full attention.

'But, unlike Muldoon, I had to leave school when I was thirteen.'

'Why didn't you stay on at school?' I asked.

'Well,' he paused, thinking how best to explain, 'my father was finding it hard to make enough money. We were more or less in poor straights.'

Mum nodded. 'Your dad didn't even have any shoes to wear to school,' she said. 'He used to walk to school in bare feet.'

'No shoes?' I said, disbelievingly.

'Lots of kids didn't have shoes in those days,' dad said. 'As each child in the family grew old enough, we had to forego any further education, leave school, and find a job to help the family budget.'

The thought of having to leave school and find a job at thirteen horrified me. 'So what job did you get?'

'Oh, I found various temporary jobs working in grocery shops and boot maker shops. None of them were much fun,' he said, sounding as though he hadn't really minded all that much.

It seemed amazing to me that he had been so accepting of this situation.

'Eventually I found a job working for R & W Hellaby, the butchers. I worked there for about three or four years as a shop man,' he said momentarily lost in reflection. Then he smiled. 'I really enjoyed the customers. I had my own butcher's round. I rode a butcher's bike with a small wheel and a big basket to deliver our rounds.'

They were happy memories of a carefree time before the world was consumed by war. Dad had been happy enough with his job as a butcher boy, but his true passion as a teenager was cycling. He and his brothers joined the Manukau Cycling Club and were soon riding great distances. He was talented too, winning some major races. He began to dream of even bigger cycling success. Some of the older boys he rode with represented New Zealand at the Empire Games and some even at the Olympics. Inspired by leading New Zealand athletes like Jack Lovelock, winner of the 1500m at the 1936 Berlin Olympics, he dared to dream that someday he might do the same. It was a time where participation in sport and recreation was booming in New Zealand. Huge crowds turned out to cheer at sporting events. For those at home, the advent of radio broadcasting now brought the atmosphere and excitement directly into the living room. Growing up in this climate, sport became very important to my father.

As well as enjoying the successes he had with cycling, he revelled in his long training rides around New Zealand, pedalling to places he otherwise wouldn't have been able to get to. He was a teenager on a bicycle having his first taste of freedom, and he loved it. Free to go wherever he wanted, he was hooked: on cycling and on freedom. Discovering new places and possibilities on his bike seemed to kick start a lifelong interest in the world around him. All through his life, my father kept a close eye on international affairs. Even as young as 19, he seemed to be able to foresee where things could be leading. Before the outbreak of war in 1939, he was only too well aware that war may be imminent and had contemplated volunteering in the event of a war. He knew he didn't want to wait until a war progressed to the point where he would almost certainly be conscripted into the army. Having been born just over a year after the First World War ended, he had grown up hearing graphic stories of war, including tales about his Uncle James who had died at Gallipoli. Dad always said that life in the trenches had been so well described, and he was under no illusion about the life of an infantryman. He made up his mind that in the event of war he would put his cycling dreams on hold and volunteer for the Air Force. The war in the air was where he thought he would fight.

Considering the interest and excitement associated with flying at the time, it's not hard to understand why my father and so many of his contemporaries sought to serve in the Air Force. They had grown up reading *Biggles* and making model airplanes. Boys dreamed of flying the aircraft they'd seen at air pageants. It was aviation's golden age starring pioneers like Kingsford Smith and Jean Batten. I don't suppose my father had heard too many horror stories about air wars. With his childhood sandwiched between the two World Wars, he wasn't exactly naive to the hardships of war, but I doubt he was aware of the emerging reality of an air battle, given the rapid advances in aircraft technology taking place at the time.

Our attitudes to war are in part shaped by the times we live in. For me, growing up during the cold war in the aftermath of the wars in Vietnam and Korea, I was strongly influenced by the anti-war sentiment around me. Studying books like *All Quiet on the Western Front* and *Hiroshima,* in high school English, deepened my anti-war resolve. When I asked my peers their views on war, we seemed to be products of time and place. One friend described herself as a 'pacifist feminist', another identified with conscientious objectors. We all felt enormously proud to be from 'Nuclear-Free New Zealand'. Of course the times were different for dad growing up in the late 1930s in the shadow of the Great War as the world lurched inevitably closer towards the greatest war the world had ever known.

* * *

Now 19 years old, my father stayed up late on Sunday 3 September 1939, listening to the wireless. I imagine the whole family waited apprehensively around the wireless that evening. They may have debated the ramifications of Germany invading Poland two days earlier, the air thick with smoke as some puffed on cigarettes. As the BBC's live broadcast from London finally commenced, my father turned up the volume and listened intently.

'This morning,' British Prime Minister Neville Chamberlain began, 'the British Ambassador in Berlin handed the German government a final note, stating that unless we heard from them, by 11 o'clock, that they were prepared at once to withdraw their troops from Poland, a state of war would exist between us.' The radio crackled. Then came the statement everyone most feared. 'I have to tell you now that no such undertaking has been received and that, consequently, this country is at war with Germany.'

There it was. It was shocking news, but my father wasn't entirely surprised. Like many, he had been fairly sure that war was inevitable. As Chamberlain's words slowly sunk in, my grandparents must have thought back to the First World War, and the brother who had never come back. They had already lived through the death and destruction of that war; now they stood on the precipice of another.

At 11.30pm that evening, the acting prime minister of New Zealand, Peter Fraser, issued a statement confirming New Zealand was now at war: 'New Zealand is ready to play her full part in the fight for democracy, justice, and freedom…In the task that lies ahead much will be expected of everyone, and I know that every man and woman in the Dominion will play his or her part.'

The following morning, my father pored over the daily newspapers, devouring everything he could about the impending war. One article quoted the Australian prime minister: 'The essence of democracy is to dignify the individual human being, and give him, whether rich or poor, the right to his place in the community and the right to a happy, prosperous, and contented life.' There was also a transcript of His Majesty the King's empire broadcast in which he had spoken about liberty, justice, sovereignty, world order and peace, calling his people at home and across the sea to make the cause their own. They were mighty ideals. From his remote island across the seas, my father received the call. He stood up, ready and willing to serve. Even if it might ultimately cost him his life, they were, he felt, principles worth fighting for.

They were certainly principles that were impossible to ignore. Political and media announcements regularly invoked the cause of freedom. A newspaper cutting dated 1940 from my father's box of keepsakes illustrates the patriotic journalistic style of the day:

New Zealand's Part in Freedom's Cause
Proud of her flying men, New Zealand is making an invaluable contribution to the Empire's resources in air warfare. Already 10,000 of her sons have volunteered... The Dominion is giving liberally of men and money to the Empire's fighting Forces. New Zealanders are united in high resolve to be partners in the great adventure–the Empire's fight for Freedom.

The great adventure. I couldn't help but wonder if my father thought it would be a great adventure in September 1939 when he decided to volunteer for war. He had no way of knowing the devastation that was to follow. More than sixty million people would lose their lives. The atrocity of the Holocaust and the dropping of the atom bomb would change the world forever.

Within days, the Air Department in Wellington called for volunteers for the Royal Air Force (RAF) and Royal New Zealand Air Force (RNZAF). 'Pilots, air gunners and observers are wanted and no previous flying experience is necessary,' the newspapers reported.

Candidates must not be less than seventeen and a half years old, but under twenty-eight years, they must be unmarried, able to the pass the prescribed medical examination and educated up to the standard of the school certificate or university entrance examination. Candidates accepted will be trained in New Zealand, and if selected for overseas service will be granted free passages to the United Kingdom.

My father wasted no time in volunteering. His years of competitive cycling meant he was fit, strong and healthy. His first application was rejected however, because he did not meet the educational requirements.

Many intelligent young men during the Great Depression hadn't had the chance to complete their high school education. But my father was undeterred. He knew he had the academic ability and refused to sit back and accept rejection. Dad told us that he 'reapplied rather forcefully,' stating his case for selection. Knowing my father's stubborn determination in the face of a hurdle, I am not surprised he was accepted the second time. After passing a rigorous physical examination, he officially joined the Air Force.

At the outbreak of war, the RNZAF was inundated with young men wanting to serve. Even as the war progressed and attrition rates were high, the Air Force, unlike the Army, never had to resort to conscription. Men were filled with patriotic duty and the spirit of adventurous youth, perhaps not fully comprehending that war, at times, could be a ghastly nightmare. My father, like so many others, was only too eager to head off to war.

Chapter 3

'The OE'

Oh, to be in England
Now that April 's there,

Robert Browning

By March 1940, my father had completed his initial training with the RNZAF. Given a few days leave, he headed home to pack his bags and say farewell to his friends and family. Back in the easy familiarity of the family home in Mt Albert, he couldn't afford to get too comfortable. He would soon be boarding a ship bound for the other side of the world – and war. Whether he knew it or not, he was about to embark on a life-changing journey, one that would threaten his very existence.

His parents and siblings were keen to hear all about his new life in the Air Force. He had just completed four weeks training at Weraroa near Levin, followed by four weeks at Ohakea Flying Station. Describing his first impressions of life in the military, my father admitted that it had been a bit of shock to the system in the beginning, with so many classes and exams to undertake.

'We had to swot really hard,' he told his family, remembering how he had initially puzzled over trigonometry and logarithms and struggled to remember the ninety parts of the Lewis gun by heart. 'Training makes you one step better than the enemy.' That was the philosophy.

'And we had to shape up too. We got into trouble for having an untidy dormitory in the first week,' he said. 'But once we got used to the discipline, we actually started to enjoy the life, strangely enough.'

His family and friends hung on his every word, especially when he described the thrill of his first flight in a Vickers Vincent biplane. 'We had a Lewis gun swivel mounted on the side of the open cockpit. You had to be careful not to shoot your own tail off.'

Everyone marvelled at how adventurous it sounded.

'Sometimes we'd get a bit crook up there,' he confessed. But he thought better of telling them about the time an aircraft had attempted to drop a parachute with a dummy in it. When the parachute had failed to open, the dummy had slammed into the ground making a frighteningly large hole.

* * *

In no time his leave was over. A large crowd gathered at the Auckland Railway Station to see him off. He only had a few minutes with his well-wishers before it was time to board the train. His good friend handed him a note that he would keep for a lifetime. Scribbled in pencil, it said, *Dear Ian, Best wishes to you on your great adventure. Buck.* Did people really think that war was going to be a great adventure? Or did it simply afford them a degree of comfort to couch it that way? I wonder how my nana was feeling as the first of her five sons headed off to war, especially having experienced the loss of her brother. Did she study her son's face intently, etching it into her memory in case she never set eyes on him again? Or did she refuse to even countenance the possibility?

Everyone waved furiously as the train pulled out of the station. As the waving crowd slowly disappeared from view, my father sat down in the knowledge that a great journey had just begun. *Farewell Auckland. Au Revoir, till we meet again,* he penned, into his diary. I'm not sure if he was trying to be optimistic or whether he felt quite certain he would return. Had he really felt as though he was going on a great adventure – an exciting journey with a mission?

Today, many New Zealanders head overseas for an extended overseas working holiday in their early twenties. In fact it's become such a common phenomenon that we Kiwis have an expression for it: the 'OE'. It stands for Overseas Experience. After graduating, many Kiwis make their way to London or other parts of the world for their OE. It's a rite of passage. My father's OE began in 1940 as he boarded the SS *Akaroa*. He and his Air Force companions were about to spend nearly seven weeks journeying to England as first class passengers. Of course, it wasn't really an OE. The expression hadn't even been coined yet, but my father's war began with an extraordinary voyage to the other side of the world.

The first group of New Zealand airmen departed New Zealand on 23 March 1940. The SS *Akaroa* sailed unceremoniously out of Lyttleton Harbour at 4.50pm, watched by only a handful of people on the wharf. With mixed feelings the men watched the ebbing shores of New Zealand's South Island. Not much was said as they stood on the deck, staring at the receding mountains silhouetted by the sinking sun. Even though they were excited by what lay ahead, it was hard not to anticipate the thrill of New Zealand appearing on the horizon again one day. Perhaps it was just as well the men didn't know that the odds of them seeing New Zealand again were heavily stacked against them. Hungry for adventure, able and willing to serve their country, they sailed on into the blue yonder as their homeland gradually faded from view. *Farewell New Zealand. Who knows what adventures await me*, my father wrote in his diary that evening.

Apart from PT in the morning, the days were largely free for them to do whatever they fancied. Deck quoits, golf, tennis and croquet were all on offer. My father liked to fill in the time by playing draughts, swimming in the 'fine tiled pool' and going to the pictures at the ship's cinema. With a cabin steward, deck steward, and dining steward all at their disposal, the men were extremely well looked after, enjoying delicious meals and brilliant sunshine day after day. Dad always left me with the impression that he'd loved every minute of this boat trip. Reading his diary I began to better understand why. It sounds like the journal of any young man having a great time on his OE. There is no sense of the war that was to follow this idyllic journey on the Pacific Ocean, through the Panama Canal and across the Atlantic to England.

25 March 1940 – Started PT at seven. Breakfast at 8.30. Beautifully fine weather, sea calm. Played deck games all morning. Cup of leaf tea at eleven. Lunch at one. Played draughts till got cleaned up. Had a workout in the gym… Dinner at 7pm, coffee in lounge. Strolled on deck, watching moon.

26 March 1940 – PT. Played deck golf after breakfast. Deck tennis, quoits etc. Took some snaps of the boys. Took a ticket in tote, which was won by L P Russell. Played draughts with Russell. Cleaned him up. Then cleaned him up at deck golf. Workout in the gym… Had tea. Retired.

Together with his good mates, airmen Les Russell, Ivan 'Robby' Robinson and Robert 'Mac' McChesney, my father passed the time much like this, week after week. It was a welcome respite after their disciplined weeks of training and study since joining the Air Force. Travelling incognito as civilians, they could have been excused for forgetting there was even a war on. After whiling away the first week on the Pacific, surrounded by little more than the deep blue sea, the men spotted a large island on the horizon.

31 March 1940 – Lovely weather. Sighted Pitcairn 10.00am arrived 3.00pm. Islanders came out in boats selling fruit and souvenirs. They are a motley crew. Had a yarn with one named Anderson Warren. Seemed a quite decent chap. Pitcairn Island not very big and very barren looking, practically surrounded by cliffs. Sea very calm and blue. Saw a school of flying fish… Oranges are the best I have tasted, the green type.

When airmen, on subsequent voyages of the *Akaroa* to Britain, saw islanders paddling out to the ship wearing pullovers and scarves made of Air Force blue, they guessed the men who had gone ahead of them on this journey had traded their surplus clothes for fruit. Perhaps my father traded his spare woollies for green oranges with Anderson Warren. For many of the men, Pitcairn was their first taste of another country and culture, the first of many eye-opening experiences to come as they journeyed across the globe. As the equator approached, the men feasted on a continuous supply of ice cream and pineapples. Overnight they rested their tanned bodies on deck chairs to survive the heat. Everyone agreed it was, so far, a most remarkable trip. In keeping with military tradition, a line crossing initiation took place as they crossed the equator.

9 April 1940 – Father Neptune's day. Crossed the equator today. Held a ceremony. Highest court placed judgment on us, (Lewis gun crew) for being in possession of an unlicensed gun. The penalty was horrid medicine, then we were whitewashed then hosed down. After we were done we grabbed King Neptune and treated him to some of his own medicine. For this we got certified.

One of the only wartime photos that dad ever showed me was of their equator crossing hijinks. They looked to be having a riotous time. Everyone in the photo was drenched and euphoric as they spiritedly acted out a timeless tradition. Along with their memorable ceremony at the equator, another highlight of the voyage that dad would occasionally recall was passing through the Panama Canal. It had clearly made quite an impression on him.

11 April 1940 – Sighted Panama at 7.00am. It was about 150 miles off. Passed a lot of islands in Panama Bay, also many strange birds. Some ugly, and some very beautifully coloured ones. Arrived out in stream at 5.00pm. Berthed at Balboa about 7.30pm. City looked great all lit up. Had some trouble about going ashore. Three of us got caught in the attempt. But a lot got away with it. Had a long argument with Mr Edwards. Eventually we went to bed at 1.30pm.

12 April 1940 – Left Balboa at 9.00am. Entered first lock at 9.30am and were lifted 30 feet then passed into other locks in the same way. Water pumped from one lock to another by gravity. Passed through the lakes, which is a huge affair about 50 miles long with dense jungle on all fringes. Saw a crocodile and an anteater. Marvellous scenery. Passed through last lock, where we dropped about 40 feet and passed on into the Caribbean Sea. Sailed on bound for Curacao. Water very blue and hot as blazes. Feeling great.

Mr Edwards was feeling a little more generous when they landed at Curacao a few days later, permitting all the men to go ashore for a swim this time.

15 April 1940 – Woke up early in the morning to find we were near a large city, the capital of Curacao. Picked up a pilot and went round to a bay to refuel. Mr Edwards kindly let us go ashore for a swim. Not sound swimming pool, half rotted away and we had to keep a lookout for sharks. Water was very warm and salty. Saw a lot of brilliantly coloured fish. Then had a rummage around the beach. There were plenty of sea eggs to be seen and also some very interesting crystallized shells. Water very clear. One could see to up to about 40 feet. We then went for a walk in the hills. Saw some lizards that change colour to suit their surroundings. They move with amazing rapidity. Later on we saw the world's smallest bird with blue and green plumage about the size of a large butterfly, with a sharp beak... Island very barren. No rain has fallen there for two years.

It was just as well the men had no real idea of what lay ahead. If they had known that within months some of them would find themselves in burning planes that were plummeting to the ground in fiery tailspins, it may have been hard to enjoy their tropical adventure. For four weeks the boys had been having a glorious international vacation, but as they headed north towards Halifax in Canada, summer abandoned the days. About the same time Germany was in the throes of celebrating the Fuhrer's fifty-first birthday, my father's ship sailed into stormy weather. One week they had been swimming in tropical Caribbean waters, the next, rain, fog and heavy seas kept them inside as the wind howled around the ship.

22 April 1940 – Woke up to roll and lurch of ship. Very cold temperature, snowing outside. Shipping some heavy seas. Arrived in the harbour at midday, anchored in stream then went into inner basin where we will anchor until the convoy leaves Halifax. Weather bitterly cold.

Originally the plan had been for the men to undergo advanced training in Halifax. They were to be the first draught to inaugurate the Empire Air Training Scheme – a programme set up shortly after war broke out to assist with the supply of some 50,000 aircrew required by Britain each year. However, plans for this contingent of pilots, gunners and observers changed suddenly, such was the urgent requirement for them in England.

On 26 April 1940 the 38th trans-Atlantic convoy departed Halifax, the SS *Akaroa* among the forty-three ships that followed one another for mutual protection. Convoy records officially listed the cargo on the *Akaroa* as 'refrig, general'. Other ships in the convoy were recorded to be carrying crude oil, lumber, wheat, grain, molasses, diesel, benzene, sugar, petrol, cotton, steel, scrap iron, whale oil and phosphates: commodities that would contribute to the million tons of imported material Britain required each week to survive and fight the war. The convoy ships were now journeying into dangerous waters. With the Germans intent on disrupting the flow of British merchant shipping, the long-running Battle of the Atlantic was already underway. If my father had been able to forget he was bound for war while cruising through the tropics, travelling in convoy would remind him. As they headed out into the Atlantic, they faced their first real threat to life and limb.

Only one day out of Halifax, the convoy ran into thick fog and the ships struggled to stay together. Gradually the *Akaroa* lost sight of the other ships. She went back and forward numerous times attempting to relocate the convoy. Seas were rough and the blanketing fog came and went, making for treacherous conditions. The occasional mournful sound of a foghorn echoed in the distance. After days of fruitless searching, it became apparent that they were not going to find the convoy. They were completely on their own. The men were only too well aware that German U-boats and Luftwaffe bombers posed a grave threat to their safety. *We are easy meat for a sub now*, my father acknowledged in his diary. A total of twenty-three ships in the final convoy records were listed as having straggled. It was uncommon for so many ships to fail to keep in convoy, but the unusually dense fog made it impossible for them to stay together.

All alone now, the SS *Akaroa* headed for England. A roster was set up for the men to undertake lookout duties. My father never forgot his dangerous trip across the Atlantic. He described it to me one day, prompted by a storm that raged around us, though no storm ever came close to the weather he had experienced in 1940 on his way to war.

'You would never believe the ferocity of the Atlantic gale we ran into on our way to England,' he told me, appearing to be right back in the heart of the storm as he painted an otherworldly picture of mayhem on the seas. He had thoroughly enjoyed it, he said, explaining that by the time they reached the Atlantic, he had his 'sea legs'. The thrill of this monster gale had left him with an exhilarating memory he seemed to enjoy reliving from time to time. This and other dramatic wartime memories must have been stirred whenever he played, as he liked to, the Naval hymn, *Eternal Father, Strong to Save*.

The upside to having lost the convoy was the *Akaroa* could resume travelling at its full speed instead of at the slower convoy pace. From my father's lookout post he saw plenty of trawlers and fishing boats about. Nearing Europe, they passed an outward-bound convoy of about twenty ships at sunrise one morning. Relieved to be approaching their final destination, it looked as though they would make it safely to England. One boat in the convoy that left Halifax the following week was not so fortunate. The *Clairy* was bombed and subsequently sunk, such was the risk of travel on the Atlantic at the time.

The men awoke on 9 May 1940 to find they were in the English Channel. They passed the gleaming white cliffs of Dover, and the towns of Ramsgate and Margate as they rounded the southeast corner of England. Soon my father would become very familiar with this heavily bombarded area while stationed at RAF Manston in the months ahead. Sailing on up the Thames, the SS *Akaroa* berthed at Tilbury Docks, east of London. As my father prepared to disembark from the ship that had been his home for nearly seven weeks, he looked around at the airmen he had shared this memorable voyage with. Along with Robby, Les and Mac, he had made some lifelong friends during the trip. Soon the group would be split up and posted to different squadrons all over England, not knowing what their respective fates would be; whether they would survive the war nor if they would ever see each other again. They stepped off the beautiful *Akaroa* and into the unknown.

* * *

By now, my father had journeyed halfway around the world. And there were still many cosmopolitan experiences yet to come; but, having shadowed him this far, I was starting to see why he had always been so worldly. The older man I knew wasn't a great traveller, preferring the solitude of his garden and the company of birds. But seeing the world at 20 had clearly made quite an impression on him, providing him with an international perspective and an outward looking focus that remained with him for life.

Nobody inspected their bags as they passed through customs at Tilbury. They took the train to London and then went by truck to Uxbridge. The men arrived at RAF Uxbridge just as the war was about to intensify. The very next day Winston Churchill became the prime minister of Britain, and Germany began its offensive against France, Belgium, Luxembourg and the Netherlands. The so-called Phoney War was over. The arrival of the New Zealand airmen was timely; they would soon be much in demand. But initially, the RAF had far more pressing things to deal with than figure out what to do with the newly arrived New Zealanders. RAF Uxbridge, tasked with despatching personnel to and from units in Northern France, was stretched to capacity with the Battle of France having just begun. Staff at the station were processing around 2,500 new and experienced servicemen per week. It is little wonder that my father described things at RAF Uxbridge as somewhat chaotic when they arrived.

9 May 1940 – Settled down in barracks. Beds hard as nails made of iron. Meals were something terrible. Tonight we had to eat with our fingers and drink out of plates.

After enjoying first class passage on the *Akaroa*, this was quite a different life to the one they had become accustomed to. The German invasion of France and the Low Countries proceeded rapidly in the following days. A few days into the Battle of France, Churchill delivered the first of his

major speeches* to the House of Commons. In it, he said, '... I have
nothing to offer but blood, toil, tears and sweat.... You ask, what is our
aim? I can answer in one word: Victory. Victory at all costs – Victory in
spite of all terror ...' My father was inspired. He had come to provide
his blood, toil, tears and sweat. He had come to play his part in ensuring
victory. And in time, as we know, there would be victory. But my father's
toil and sweat were not required just yet. For the first few weeks the boys
were largely left to their own devices at Uxbridge on the outskirts of
London, as the RAF focused on the escalating crisis in Europe. Leave
was readily available and, whenever possible, my father and his mates
took the opportunity to explore the famous sights of London.

> *16 May 1940 – Went to London in afternoon via tubes. Went to New
> Zealand House for information and mail. Then went and had a look
> at Buckingham Palace, St James Palace, Green Park, Hyde Park,
> Trafalgar Square, Whitehall, Piccadilly Circus, Westminster Abbey,
> Big Ben... Went ice-skating.*

The OE hadn't quite finished. Despite the grave situation developing
on the other side of the English Channel, the boys were having
rather a good time. They enjoyed having some meals at the famed
Lyons Corner Houses. Pleased to be avoiding the terrible food in the
Sergeant's Mess at Uxbridge, they ordered something more appetising
from the 'Nippys'– the waitresses who nipped around in their spotless
black and white maid-like uniforms with matching hats. With the
perspective of a young, wide-eyed antipodean, who had grown up
in the Depression and never even eaten out, these bustling Art Deco
styled restaurants, with musicians playing, were very special places. He
talked about them occasionally, one of the happier wartime memories

---

* Reproduced with permission of Curtis Brown, London on behalf of The Estate of
Winston S. Churchill. © The Estate of Winston S. Churchill.

he readily shared. He also got a kick out of visiting clubs such as the *Empire Rendezvous* near Trafalgar Square, a place where 'officers and men from the dominions were welcome to go for reading, writing, light refreshments and information.' On their first visit to the *Empire Rendezvous*, the Kiwi airmen were treated with great hospitality. They were invited to stay with Lords after the war, and given free seats to the revue *Me and My Girl*. I wonder if the men were treated to a few drinks this particular evening, because on the way home they got lost. After wandering about for three hours, unable to find their way in the blackout, they finally chanced on the drome. They expected to be in a lot of trouble, but with so much else going on at RAF Uxbridge, their arrival back in the wee small hours was overlooked.

The first few months of my father's 1940 diary gave me a taste of who he had been before he was touched by war. This carefree lad who had 'promenaded' on the decks of the *Akaroa* and roamed the streets of London in the wee small hours, wasn't someone I could easily associate with my father. The man I knew was far more serious and contemplative than this happy-go-lucky adventurer. Despite their exploits in London, the men wouldn't have been able to forget the real reason they were there. Events in Europe were worsening. British Expeditionary Force (BEF) troops arriving back from France and Belgium were processed at Uxbridge. My father saw many returning soldiers who, not surprisingly under the circumstances, were looking rather 'unkempt and unshaven.'

24 May 1940 Constant stream of B.E.F. returning from evacuated areas in Belgium and France. Left all kit behind. Germans bombing and gunning hell out of them. Went out for a nice peaceful ramble. Heard distant boom of guns. Getting nearer.

Within days the Dunkirk evacuation was in full flight and many more weary and dishevelled soldiers continued to arrive at the camp at

Uxbridge. Hearing some of their dramatic tales first-hand, my father was vicariously transported to the hell on earth that was the western front at Dunkirk. It was his first taste of war. After spending four weeks at RAF Uxbridge with little to do, my father was pleased to learn that he had finally been posted to Duxford aerodrome for further training. As he was packing to leave Uxbridge in early June, Churchill gave his next major speech to the House of Commons, describing the way the Germans had overrun Holland, Belgium and northern France. My father, like so many of his peers, was moved by Churchill's stirring rhetoric. Even decades later, dad would occasionally say, with a Churchillian tone and a hint of a smile, 'We shall *never, surrender.*' Fired up by Churchill, he couldn't have been happier on his first morning at Duxford Aerodrome, now that his work was finally about to begin.

> *5 June 1940 – Rolled out with a smile at 7.15. Weather fine. Had a good look at the Defiants and their turrets from which we will be operating. The system is four guns converging on harmonization point. Works by lever resembling joysticks. Received complete outfit of flying gear almost enough to fill another bag. Knocked off at 4 o'clock. Robby and Les went up for a flight after tea. They reckon it's great.*

Together with one of his best pals Robby, my father spent his first week happily immersed in training, getting to grips with manipulating the turret. After his first flight in a Defiant, he thought it certainly lived up to its name. But he was to experience the tragedy of war only one week after arriving at Duxford, when Robby was on an ill-fated flight with a Scottish pilot.

> *11 June 1940 – Half a dozen of the boys went up for a flip this afternoon and one crashed and burst into flames. Pilot Officer Hutchison was killed. Robby was the gunner and had a very narrow escape, being just*

*dragged out before the flames reached him. He is severely cut about the
face and has a broken jaw.*

My father must surely have known when he volunteered for war nine
months earlier that his life, and that of those around him, would be
in jeopardy. But I don't imagine it made it any easier to see one of his
best friends all cut up, having almost lost his life. Thankfully, Robby
was alive – for the time being anyway – but he had come perilously
close to losing his life before he'd even seen a combat theatre. With
more gunners than were required in the training unit at 264 Squadron
in Duxford, the next day my father and some of the other Kiwis were
reposted to 5 Operational Training Unit (OTU), Aston Downs to
undertake a comprehensive three-week gunnery course on Bristol
Blenheims. Before departing, he went to visit Robby. Finding that he
was still anaesthetised, my father was disappointed to have to leave his
injured friend behind without even a good-bye.

* * *

At RAF Aston Downs, my father closely followed developments in
Europe. He noted on 16 June: *War situation getting very grave.* He
listened intently to Winston Churchill deliver another charismatic
speech in the House of Commons on 18 June 1940. Churchill
commented on the fall of France, and pointed out the prospects for
invasion by Germany: 'I expect that the Battle of Britain is about to
begin .... Let us therefore brace ourselves to our duties, and so bear
ourselves that, if the British Empire and its Commonwealth last for a
thousand years, men will still say, "This was their finest hour."'

Still worried about Robby, and with the risk of a Nazi invasion
increasing by the day, my father wrote in his diary that evening with a
heavy heart.

18 June 1940 – Spent morning on Vickers G.O. gun, stripping and assembling it. Took notes all afternoon. After France's capitulation I am wondering when I shall get home back to NZ again. Someday maybe and perhaps never. I'm in a pensive mood tonight.

He had underlined 'perhaps never'. This is the first time he sounds anything other than chipper in his diary. He had been in England just over a month, and his training was almost complete. With the Battle of Britain about to begin, it seemed to be dawning on him that this 'adventure' may be going to be more challenging than perhaps he had anticipated. The OE was well and truly over.

Chapter 4

'Fate, it seems, had taken a hand'

I know that I shall meet my fate
Somewhere among the clouds above;

W.B. Yeats

y father stared out the vehicle window at the gardens and
farmland of Kent and admired the immense fields of
purple lavender. Having earned his Air Gunner's badge
and been promoted to Sergeant at the end of the three-week course at
Aston Downs, the time had come for his first permanent posting, and
he was on his way to join his new squadron. He was looking forward to
settling down in one place. The voyage to England had been flanked on
either side by training courses at several different airbases, keeping him
on the move for six months. There had even been a brief extra stop this
week at RAF Northolt as a result of a mix-up that would long remain
a source of amusement for him. A few days earlier, at the entrance to
Northolt airbase, he had handed his Air Gunner's papers to the guard,
expecting to be ushered in to join his new squadron. While the guard
examined his papers, my father took a deep breath, trying not to feel
like a 20-year-old all alone on the other side of the world. His mates,
the airmen he had journeyed with from New Zealand, had all been
posted to different squadrons across the country and he was now very
much on his own.

'What are you going to do?' the guard asked him curtly.

'What do you mean?'

'Are you going to sit on the tail?'

My father hadn't known what to make of this. He'd been told to report to RAF Northolt and here he was.

'This is a *Spitfire* squadron,' the guard said impatiently.

Clearly there had been some mistake. A Spitfire squadron wouldn't require an air gunner. My father had no alternative but to wait a few days until word came from the Air Ministry advising that he was in fact to join the Blenheim squadron at RAF Manston.

Now almost at his new airbase, right in the southeast corner of England, he inhaled deeply, trying to smell the salt on the air as they rounded a corner and a glimpse of the English Channel appeared on the horizon. Driving along the slowly climbing approach road to RAF Manston, he wondered what life with 600 Squadron was going to be like. Entering the gates, he surveyed the large airbase that was about to become his new home. On the far side of the wide all-grass airfield were buildings and hangars. A railway line ran along beside them. Ground crew were working on the aircraft parked near the hangars. Before he could take in much more, an air raid warning wailed unexpectedly. The driver hastily pulled over by an air raid shelter. As they exited the vehicle, a thundering noise drew their eyes skyward. Four German Messerschmitt Bf 109s (Me 109s) were hurtling overhead and Spitfires were about to attack them. My father stared wide-eyed into the sky. It was the first aerial combat that he had ever witnessed, although it certainly wouldn't be the last.

Later in life, dad gave a sketchy description of what played out above him as he arrived at Manston. In his memory, the Spitfires managed to get the better of the German aircraft. Much to his amazement, two of them crashed to a horrifying and fiery end right in front of him. But he finished his anecdote almost nonchalantly, saying: 'So that was our baptismal fire as it were.' He didn't make it sound like the big deal it must have been at the time, but I guess that was with hindsight. While it had been a dramatic start to his time at Manston, it wouldn't be long until his 'baptismal fire' would pale into insignificance. The very next morning would herald the beginning of what would become known as the Battle of Britain. His timing was impeccable.

* * *

My father was up at dawn on his first morning at RAF Manston. Fired up and ready to begin his official service, he needed to take care of some administrative matters first. He set out to find the Orderly Room among the main group of buildings nestled in the northwest corner of the airbase. No sooner had he begun to make his way there than the air raid siren once again bellowed forth. He looked around, quickly taking in his new surroundings, his heart rate beginning to rise. With the siren wailing, he wasted no time following a group of men into a nearby air raid shelter. And so began life at Manston, stuck below ground for one and a half hours. At least it gave him an opportunity to get to know some of his new squadron colleagues while they waited for the all clear.

'Just arrived at Hell's Corner?' one of the chaps asked him.

'Is that what you call it here?'

Everyone nodded.

'It's about right too,' my father said, recalling the dogfight he had witnessed on arrival the previous day.

While they talked, someone told him that a bomb had fallen 50 yds from the hut they were sleeping in a few nights ago. *It's red hot here,* he wrote in his diary later that day. *Just what I wanted.* RAF Manston was the airbase closest to the enemy coast during the Battle of Britain and its vulnerability at this geographical location wasn't lost on anyone. During the First World War, Manston had begun life as a Royal Naval Air Station, with four underground hangars and barracks for 3,000 men. Chatting to the others, he learned that 600 (City of London)

Squadron was the only squadron currently based there, though other squadrons used Manston as a forward operating base during the day. Everyone was very welcoming, but my father was a bit disappointed to learn that no other New Zealanders were, as yet, based at Manston.

Finally they were given the all clear to vacate the shelter. Famished, he headed to the Sergeant's Mess for breakfast and was pleased with what he found. Having been at a few RAF bases in his short time in England, this was easily the best Mess he'd experienced so far. He happily helped himself to some grapefruit. It's just like old times on board the *Akaroa*, he thought. With his stomach pleasantly full, he took a stroll around the base and walked through picturesque Manston village with the church of St Catherine at its heart. He paused at the First World War memorial in front of the church and admired the ivy-covered houses. Behind the church was the village school, which had been closed at the outbreak of war. Now it housed the NAAFI – the Navy, Army and Air Force Institute – where servicemen could purchase goods.

That morning, six 74 Squadron Spitfires were scrambled from Manston and managed to harm a German Dornier escorted by numerous fighters. Two aircraft crash-landed on return. Initially comprised of a series of air battles over convoys in the English Channel, the first phase of the Battle of Britain was just beginning. Later that day, Air-Vice Marshal Keith Park visited RAF Manston. Dad was always proud that this extraordinary New Zealander's leadership was acknowledged as crucial to winning the Battle of Britain. After spending his first day at Manston becoming familiar with the base and its procedures, my father wandered over to the large buildings near their long, narrow sleeping quarters. He was pleased to discover a well kitted out gymnasium and an indoor swimming pool. He wrapped up his first day by 'indulging' in a swim after tea.

* * *

Having settled in at RAF Manston, it was soon time for my father's first patrol. As the hour loomed on 13 July, I imagine he may have been feeling apprehensive in anticipation of his first official flight. But he was certainly in no doubt about the reason he was there. The British Foreign Secretary Viscount Halifax had summed it up perfectly in a broadcast address: 'We are fighting in defence of freedom. We are fighting for peace… We are defending the rights of all nations to live their own lives.' And my father was well and truly ready to get on with the job he was trained for.

Pilot Officer Ritchie skilfully took their Bristol Blenheim into the air. The Blenheim 1F, fitted with top-secret radar, had been converted from a bomber to a night fighter with a pack of four Browning machine guns mounted underneath. For my father, positioned in the turret, it was time to put all of his training into practice. They flew for eighty-five minutes over the southeast coast. It took awhile to become accustomed to the aircraft's pervasive smell of hydraulic oil. Landing back at the base, my father felt a little deflated that they hadn't seen anything of note. Later that afternoon, they spent four hours confined in a shelter after the air raid warning sounded once again. Dinner was delayed. The next night, at midnight, there was another air raid warning. Amidst the panic, the men tumbled out of bed, shoved their feet into their shoes, and raced to the nearest shelter. As they huddled together in the dark below ground, they could hear the fearsome boom of German bombs raining down nearby. Fortunately no bombs fell directly on the airbase. The Luftwaffe must have been fooled by the dummy flare path that had been built on the nearby Minster marshes. Broken sleep and bombs falling nearby made the previous day's late dinner seem relatively inconsequential. But it wouldn't be long until a few misguided bombs would barely raise an eyebrow.

* * *

In the dark summer of 1940, the British Empire was all that stood between Hitler and command of Europe. As one of the Empire men who had journeyed across the seas to make the cause their own, my father could see that the situation was becoming increasingly bleak. On 16 July 1940, Hitler issued Führer Directive No 16, setting in motion preparations for a landing in Britain. He stated the aim of the operation was to eliminate England as a base from which the war against Germany could be continued and, if necessary, occupy the country completely. The following day my father recorded, *Nightly we are expecting the invasion. Rumoured for Friday now.* There was widespread concern that Britain would soon succumb to Nazi aggression. Anti-invasion measures were taken with a sense of urgency. On free evenings, my father would go into the nearby seaside towns of Ramsgate and Margate where he noticed defence preparations were underway. Exploring Ramsgate one evening, he saw many shop windows boarded up, but was pleasantly surprised when he was still able to go to the cinema.

Most days in July he was involved in patrols or air tests. Guns were cleaned and harmonized. When they were stood down from patrol duties, the Air Gunners would sometimes help to man the gun enforcements on the airbase. Anti-aircraft defences had been made of anything they had to hand, even guns salvaged from crashed aircraft. It was inevitable they would also have to spend several intermittent hours of the day in an underground air raid shelter where there was nothing else to do except have a yarn while they waited. They liked to joke that they were now 'in the final', with only themselves and the Germans left. Humour seemed to help them deal with the tough situation they faced. My father enjoyed getting to know the others. I remember him saying, as the only New Zealander in the squadron initially, he was a bit of a novelty. Everyone treated him 'rather well' and he found his colleagues very friendly. When time allowed, he enjoyed a swim in the airbase pool or took some time out with his squadron colleagues. He liked to keep abreast of how everyone was getting on. One day he noted: *At 16:00 hours the hurricanes took off and tackled some more Jerrys shooting down about four Me 109s. Nice work.* The next day he wrote, *Another good day for our fighters: bagged 14 Jerrys.*

I was surprised to see my father had used derogatory words like 'Jerry' and 'Hun'. I never heard my father utter these words. The man I knew, decades on from these diary entries, held no malice towards the German people. On the contrary, it was a regular morning at home if dad got up in the morning and said *'Haben sie gut geschlafen?'* (Did you sleep well?) He taught me to count to 100 in German when I was about 7 and thought nothing of peppering his conversation with German phrases from time to time. But with a war on and an enemy to defeat, words like Jerry and Hun were, of course, in popular usage at the time.

* * *

Crews from several squadrons were involved in defending a nearby convoy on Wednesday 24 July 1940. A massive dogfight developed over Margate and several German fighters were shot down.

Having had the base bombed several times in the brief period my father had been in Manston, and with the battle heating up, I imagine he would have been grateful for some respite when he was given a few days leave. Bound for Exeter, he spent his first night staying at the Overseas League in London and had an enjoyable time with some New Zealand soldiers he met there. At breakfast the next morning he was surprised to run into Fred Hindrup, an air gunner he had trained with at the beginning of the year in New Zealand. Fred had been on a later voyage to England and had only recently arrived. He told my father that one of the ships in his convoy had been torpedoed.

In Exeter, my father stayed with Mrs Nicholls, an elderly lady who kindly opened her home during the war to New Zealanders on leave from the Air Force. Among the happy wartime memories dad shared, Mrs Nicholls' kindness and hospitality was right at the top of the list.

27–29 July 1940 – Staying in Exeter with Mrs Nicholls. She is a dear old soul and is spoiling me… Went for a long ramble. Very peaceful round about here. Weather glorious. Set out on a ramble by motor through Devon and over Dartmoors. Visited Buckfast Abbey. Wonderful old place built by monks. I could have stayed there all day looking around. From there we went to Widdicombe of Widdicombe Fair fame. Morning tea with real Devonshire cream and jam. (Great) Then home across the huge expanse of fascinating Dartmoor moors. Very pretty with heather in bloom.

Reading my father's diary, I am struck by the contrast between being bombed in Manston one day, to wandering around Exeter like a tourist the next. Throughout his time in England during the war, this pattern repeats over and over. Periods of extreme danger were punctuated by jaunts to explore new places. He seemed to be able to exist in separate compartments – one marked 'war' and the other 'sightseeing'. I wonder whether he was ever able to really relax during periods of leave, and momentarily forget there was a war to go back and fight, or if he only saw the beautiful Devon countryside through glasses darkened by war. On his journey back to Manston, he spent another night in London, staying this time at the Victoria League Club.

1 August 1940 – Visited NZ House this morning and collected some mail. Letters from Keith, Cyril, [brothers] and Mum. Read up the latest New Zealand papers. Posted a watch to Mum. Caught train for Margate… Retired early after six days of much pleasure.

My father was straight back into work on his return. During his next patrol they flew very low over Dover. It was thrilling to approach the white cliffs from the sea, skimming over the top of them with barely a hair's breadth below. The pilots had been told to fly low over the surrounding towns on their way back into Manston to remind the locals that the RAF were in constant defence of their shores. When they returned, there was an air raid during which my father saw a Spitfire bring down an enemy aircraft. The next night a German fighter flew down extremely low over Manston and machine-gunned one of their searchlights. Right back in the thick of the Battle of Britain, the tranquil times in Exeter seemed a million miles away.

* * *

8 August 1940 wasn't a day my father ever told me about, but I doubt it was a day he ever forgot. That morning, he was preparing for a sortie in their Blenheim L8665 with Flying Officer Grice and radar operator AC1 John Warren. He had been impressed with pilot Grice when they had gone air firing a couple of weeks earlier, noting that he was an 'excellent shot'. Fresh in his mind was the order of the day that had been read aloud to units all across the country: '*Members of the Royal Air Force, the fate of generations lies in your hands,*' leaving them in no doubt of the dire importance of their task. Preparations for the patrol were well underway when my father was unexpectedly told he was required elsewhere.

'I've been asked to go and relieve the Duty Air Gunner immediately,' he said to his pilot as he headed off.

Before long, Grice and Warren had almost completed their preparations for take-off. Without my father, they needed a last minute replacement air gunner. Sergeant Keast was seconded to the job. My father would miss out on this particular patrol. Flying Officer Grice wasted no time ascending into the skies above Kent. Rising above the clouds, it wasn't long before his Blenheim was unexpectedly within range of a Luftwaffe fighter, flown by Oberleutnant Gustav Sprick of III Group, JG 26. The German fired with deathly accuracy. The Blenheim flew straight into the stream of bullets.

Newspapers subsequently reported that locals in Ramsgate saw the Blenheim appear through the clouds with black smoke streaming from its tail. As the stricken aircraft flattened out, flames began to spread along its length. Rapidly losing height, the fighter looked as though it would crash into the centre of town. Observers expected the pilot to take to his parachute, but Flying Officer Grice heroically stayed at the controls of the doomed aircraft as it descended, trying to guide it clear of the town. The burning Blenheim seemed to skim above the rooftops by mere feet, dodging a tall building before it crashed in flames into the sea, 50 yds from Ramsgate harbour. The townspeople were saved but the entire crew was killed. It was five minutes to midday.

Flying Officer Dennis Neve Grice's body was recovered and cremated at Charing Crematorium in Kent. He was 28 years old and had married nine short months earlier. 31-year-old Sergeant Francis John Keast was interred at Whitstable Cemetery. John Benjamin William Warren's body was later washed ashore in France. Only 19 years old, he was buried at Calais Southern Cemetery. My father was supposed to have been on that plane. But as he confided in his diary, *Fate, it seems, had taken a hand.* He figured somehow, inexplicably, he wasn't supposed to die that day.

Seventy-four years later, I unexpectedly came face to face with pieces of the wreckage from this crash at the RAF Manston History Museum. To be up close and personal with a propeller blade and piece of the aircraft's engine from a crash, which had nearly claimed my father, was hard to wrap my head around. If my father had died that day, I would never have been born and yet here I was, even touching a piece of the doomed Blenheim's wreckage, while Sergeant Keast had perished, no descendants ever to follow in his wake. Was he simply a victim of fate's whim? I crouched alone with this wreckage for quite some time, contemplating the mysteries of life for which there are no answers. After awhile I realised I wasn't completely alone. A Daddy-longlegs spider was exploring the wreckage too. With all the strange emotions I was grappling with in that moment, the spider almost seemed to represent my father and his life that had been preserved.

Thanks to the skill and bravery of pilot Grice, a great many lives, present and future, were saved in Ramsgate that day. In 2006, a memorial plaque was unveiled in Ramsgate acknowledging the debt of gratitude owed to this crew for deliberately steering their burning aircraft away from the town centre to prevent civilian casualties. '*The townspeople of Ramsgate will remember forever their supreme sacrifice in averting a greater disaster,*' the memorial says. Reflecting on the courage and sacrifice of the men named on the memorial, I am shocked to think how perilously close my father's name came to being engraved on it. I do wonder why my father never shared this extraordinary story with me. Incredibly, he seemed to have been plucked from the jaws of death. Was he afraid of opening Pandora's box? If he had told me this story, it may have prompted all kinds of questions about his Air Force days, questions that may have disturbed memories firmly buried in the furthest recesses of his mind. It does go some way to explaining why dad was such a fatalist. He had an incredible faith that everything would turn out okay. 'Life always works out if you let it,' he would say.

Chapter 5

'All hell let loose'

Freedom is the sure possession of those alone who have the courage to defend it.

Pericles

My father's diary entries indicate that action aplenty continued around him in the days that followed that fateful flight.

9 August 1940 – Saw some great dog fights yesterday. Spitfires shooting down Me 109s. Shot down about four. Yesterday's bag was 60 enemy aircraft shot down. Our losses were 16 fighters. Mild thrill this morning. Was up in Blenheim with no airspeed indicator. We had crash wagon all ready in case we crashed on landing. But pilot bought it down ok. Tonight we had just got into bed when bombs started dropping. Grabbed our tin hats and made for the shelter. Jerry had dropped 8 parachute flares and was letting go terrific salvos of bombs. Our squadron was up looking for the Jerrys when one of them suddenly crashed with engine trouble. The crew bailed out successfully. The sky was bright red with the burning Blenheim.

11 August 1940 – Last night went up hunting Jerrys but couldn't find any. When we landed my pilot misjudged slightly and we had a minor crash. Overshot the field and finished up in a ditch. I got well shaken up in the back but was not injured. Smashed a prop and also the tail of the kite. (Nice thrill)

12 August 1940 – Was on readiness again last night. Was up for 2½ hours hunting for bandits. It was damn cold, and didn't see any Huns. Made a good landing…

Reading my father's diary entries from these early days of the war, I am surprised by how gung-ho he sounds. He described the thrills and spills of his hair-raising experiences with the excitement and invincibility of a young lad not yet battle weary or exposed to the worst horrors of war. But it wouldn't be long before that would all change. The second phase of the Battle of Britain was just beginning. Codenamed Adlerangriff (Eagle Attack), the Luftwaffe was now moving its focus to the coastal airfields.

On Monday 12 August, a specialist German fighter-bomber unit attacked four coastal radar stations. The Germans figured that the RAF had been rendered blind. What they didn't anticipate was that most of the radar stations would be back in action within hours. But there would still be time to exploit Manston's proximity to Europe. While the radar stations were out of action, large numbers of enemy aircraft headed directly for RAF Manston. Fighter Command only learned of the approaching threat when the ominous swarm of aircraft were almost overhead.

Unaware of the impending danger, several 65 Squadron Spitfires were at Manston, about to take off on a routine patrol. It had already been an eventful morning for these airmen who had been scrambled to protect two nearby convoys where two ships had been sunk. They had returned to Manston at 11.15am to refuel and were now on the wide all grass airfield forming up to take off together, with no idea that enemy bombers were closing in. While the Spitfires were preparing for take-off, my father was sitting down to a quiet lunch in the Mess, with no reason to suspect this meal would be any different to any other he'd had at RAF Manston.

Without any warning whatsoever, a monstrous boom vibrated across the base, followed quickly by another, and another. Bombs were exploding everywhere, prompting lightning-quick responses from the men in blue. Many plunged to the ground seeking shelter, stunned by the force of the blasts. Overhead, Messerschmitt Bf 110s (Me 110s) were dive-bombing RAF Manston. At the same time, low-flying Dorniers roared overhead, bombing and strafing as they went. Numerous bombs exploded all around the 65 Squadron Spitfires as they attempted to take off. One of the pilots saw a hangar roof fly off nearby as he tried to get airborne. Miraculously, only one of the Spitfires didn't get into the air, its engine having been stopped by a bomb exploding behind it. As more and more bombs detonated, white smoke began to envelope the aerodrome. Pilots who witnessed the attack from the air wondered if the base was on fire. In fact it was only the chalk dust emanating from the many craters that now scarred the airfield.

Seeing my father's diary entry for that day, it was immediately obvious that something critical had happened. There had evidently been a great deal to record and he had written in the smallest possible scrawl.

12 August 1940 – We had word of a raid on our drome today. Sure enough, just sitting down to lunch when fifty dive-bombers attacked letting go whistling bombs. We were all flat on the floor of the mess in about a fifth of a second. Boom! Boom! Bombs were falling all around. Twelve spitfires took off as the first salvo was falling. They got safely off and brought down ten bombers. Altogether 150 bombs were dropped. Most of them fell on the runways. Three hangars were hit but there was nothing in them. One bomb burst the water main. It was all hell let loose for a while. Two people were killed.

The plethora of bombs that fell for around five minutes destroyed hangars and workshops and damaged two Blenheims. About one hundred craters punctured the grass runways and they were declared unfit for use. But, with the help of the Army, Manston was operational again by dawn the next morning. My father and his colleagues refused to be dismayed by this massive bombing raid, the first major attack on a British airbase.

Berlin claimed to have reduced Manston to ashes, a fantastic statement. They certainly messed up the landing ground, but on the whole, damage was slight. Ten of the bombs were 1000lbs and caused terrific explosions. We were all a bundle of nerves that night. Slightest noise made us jump out of our skins. Dive-bombing is sheer hell.

It was a day my father would always vividly remember. 'We really experienced the might of the German Air Force,' he recalled later in life. 'We were having lunch in the Sergeant's Mess when a bombing raid took place, which was so unexpected. With no warning whatsoever, came the deafening crash of a stick of bombs. I remember concerted dives under the tables,' he said. 'The peacetime warrant officers had rather looked down on us as "jumped up sergeants" without experience. But we were all levelled to the same grade under the tables. It was quite amusing to see these warrant officers and us "jumped up sergeants" in the same situation.' It wasn't so much the terror of experiencing the bombing raids that had stayed with him, rather their equalising effect on the hierarchy of Air Force men. Fear, it seems, didn't discriminate by rank or experience.

Two days later, numerous Me 110s again pointed their noses towards Manston. At 12.10pm, about thirty enemy planes converged on the drome. As unheralded bombs began to fall too close for comfort, my father was catapulted to his feet and began to sprint towards the nearest shelter. The young Kiwi struggled to recognise himself as he ran for his life in the shadow of a massive air battle. Putting one leg in front of the other as rapidly as he could, he dared to raise his eyes skyward. Just as he looked up, a 40mm Bofors shell, fired by airfield defences, hit a German Messerschmitt, breaking its tail off. It collided with another Messerschmitt causing both aircraft to plummet catastrophically towards the airfield. One of the German airmen aboard, Gefreiter Schank managed to bail out at 500 ft and was dragged along the ground by his chute while bombs from his own unit were falling around him. My father witnessed the breath-taking destruction of both aircraft crashing onto the drome in flames during his race to the shelter.

Crammed into sandbag slit trenches, the men knew it wouldn't just be the Germans who suffered during the raid. As bombs continued to rain down, shaking the ground, the main hangars were left blazing and a sizeable crater formed in the middle of the airfield. Several dispersals were ruined and three Blenheims on the ground were destroyed, while in nearby Manston village, two oil bombs fell. My father was beginning to understand the real meaning of the word 'war' and the way the Nazis waged it.

* * *

RAF Manston continued to be bombed in the ensuing days; my father, however, was sent to RAF Hornchurch the next evening to do night readiness. He became stuck there for a few days, after bad weather curtailed any flying. Far from seeming relieved to be away from his heavily bombarded base, his diary entries are a catalogue of complaints. *Sergeants Mess here at Hornchurch not so hot.* The next day he penned: *Nothing doing today. Bad weather again curtailed operations. I am stranded up here without any gear.* He remained unimpressed: *Very dull here. Still at Hornchurch doing nothing.* By day four he was clearly missing Manston and his belongings: *Feeling very dirty. We have very*

poor working facilities here. Don't like this place very much. Had another
air raid warning here today. But it was a fizzer.

I would have thought my father might have welcomed a few days
away from Manston and all the bombs that were wreaking havoc,
but apparently not. I'm not sure if he was aware that there had been
further attacks on Manston and few of the buildings that remained
were habitable. RAF Hornchurch may have been dull, but the situation
was far worse for those that remained at Manston. A little light relief
arrived in the middle of it all when Sergeant Alan Burdekin from 600
Squadron joined my father at Hornchurch. They filled in some time
playing billiards. English-born Alan Burdekin would emigrate to New
Zealand after the war and maintained a lifelong friendship with my
father. I well remember Alan and his wife coming to stay with us when
I was growing up. Dad and Alan talked almost non-stop about the war
and I remember being surprised by all the focus it was given for several
days. I suppose dad didn't ordinarily talk about the war a great deal.
So it seemed strange to me, with the narrow perspective of a young
teenager, to have day after day dominated by war talk. I remember
feeling glad at the time that my father wasn't normally consumed
by the war. Ironically, now I'd love to be able to ask him countless
questions about his wartime days.

264 Squadron was relocated to Hornchurch at the same time. My
father was chuffed when Les Russell and some of his other friends
from the *Akaroa* arrived. *It was great having a yarn with them. They*
have had no action and have not even been bombed. But I think they
will get all they want on Defiant Fighters. Not getting much action at
RAF Hornchurch may not have seemed so bad after the events that
followed his return to Manston that evening. Intent on wiping out
the RAF on the ground, the Luftwaffe was about to take the next
step in its plan to take airfields such as Manston, piece by piece.

22 August 1940 – Did nothing all day and after tea went back to Manston. Just walking down to Sergeants Mess when I saw the Spitfire pilots dashing out to take off. About ten minutes later, Jerry bombed the place again. No warning had been given. They set two hangars on fire. Burst another water main. After they had gone the warning went.

Miraculously no one was killed this time, although the damage to buildings and hangars was extensive. Several courageous firemen from the Margate brigade tried to save the guns and equipment from a burning armoury. Two men used air-breathing apparatus to enter the smoke filled armoury, and heroically passed the equipment out via a chain of firemen lying on their backs. All the men involved were later commended for their extraordinary valour. The next day there was only one air raid warning, *but it made us run never the less.* Thankfully, Manston wasn't bombed that day.

But it turned out to be a moment of calm before the storm.

* * *

Saturday 24 August 1940 dawned bright and sunny, signalling that the Luftwaffe would undoubtedly be coming. And they did. When warning came of approaching enemy aircraft, throngs of airmen and ground crew headed frantically towards the nearest shelter. They knew only too well the terror that was about to unfold. Though it would turn out that nothing they had experienced so far would quite prepare them for this horror day. Swarms of enemy aircraft began to repeatedly bomb Manston like never before. Many of the bombs landed squarely on buildings. Soon most of them were badly damaged, some swallowed up by the cavernous craters forming everywhere. The water mains were severed, which left them without water to douse the numerous fires that blazed furiously. The Defiants from 264 Squadron were scrambled and attempted to take off at Manston as bombs were falling. Les Russell was in one of the few aircraft that managed to get through to the enemy bombers. He and Pilot Officer Young damaged a Junkers Ju 88 and a Heinkel He 111.

Fire fighters who subsequently arrived at the drome were astounded by the devastation that awaited them. Fires burned uncontrollably across the deserted base, ripping through hangars and sleeping quarters. Pieces of plane, strewn across the airfield, were ablaze. Utter chaos reigned. Throughout the day there were three separate raids on Manston, resulting in by far the most severe damage to date. Seven people were killed. It was even worse in nearby Ramsgate, where thirty-one people were killed and dozens injured; 500 high explosive bombs and some oil incendiary bombs hit the town, destroying and damaging hundreds of houses.

After it was all over, great clouds of white dust hung over Manston and its surrounds. The bombs had penetrated the solid chalk under the thin layer of grass and soil, creating a ghostly gloom. To make matters even worse, more than 200 unexploded bombs littered the airbase. My father was lucky to survive the catastrophic raids.

24 August 1940 – Jerry has put Manston out of action. He bombed us three times. I had a very narrow escape, being blown down an air raid shelter when bombs were falling all around me. It shook me up. Bombs hit two big hangars. Direct hit on a shelter, also a lot of the barracks. Burnt down a lot of the buildings. We were in shelters all day and came away to Hornchurch about 6 o'clock. Left a mass of ruins behind. Hundreds of Jerrys were over all day long. Les Russell shot down a Heinkel 111. Had two German airmen in the Sergeant's Mess last night. Just like us they are. But they hate us.

My father's reflection about their German prisoners intrigued me. He seemed somewhat surprised to discover that they were 'just like us', but taken aback by the hatred they demonstrated. Coming face to face with your enemy must have been completely different to trying to shoot down an enemy aircraft.

I was surprised to learn about the massive bombing raids on Manston. I knew my father had been based at Manston during the Battle of Britain, but overall he was pretty reticent about his time there, scattering a few details such as the dogfight that had coincided with his arrival. I pictured any of the stories he did share in black and white because, to me, they sounded like scenes from an old war movie. Little did I know how like a dramatic movie his time at Manston had actually been. His diary entries don't really give the impression that he was highly traumatised by the bombings. But the obvious terror of being bombed day after day, and the fact that he never talked much about it, makes me think otherwise. Perhaps he summed it up best with the succinct sentence he wrote one dramatic day in August 1940: *Dive-bombing is sheer hell.*

RAF Manston holds the dubious distinction of being the RAF's most bombed airfield during the Second World War. By the end of this nightmare day, a crippled RAF Manston was removed from the map of fighter airfields and closed for all but emergency use. The Germans had been so effective in bombing Manston that there were persistent rumours that a fifth column agent had been based at the camp, secretly letting the German Air Force know when the squadrons would be most unprepared for them. To my father, this rumour certainly seemed to explain a lot. Manston would rise from the cinders (and chalk dust) in the months ahead. Operations would resume in an increasingly more offensive role. Manston would be from where Dambusters ace Sir Barnes Wallace carried out tests on the revolutionary bouncing bomb before it was famously used in the raid on Germany's Ruhr Valley. When I visited Manston, more than seventy years later, it was almost impossible to visualise how it had been during the war, or to imagine the chaos of bombs raining down. Most of the buildings from my father's time were long gone, having been burned and reduced to rubble in the August 1940 bombing raids, and there was nothing to evoke the dramas my father had experienced. The RAF Manston site became 'Manston, Kent's International Airport', for a time. Set among peaceful, rolling farmland, the occasional Boeing 747 dotted around the vast open space looked almost out of place. Air traffic controllers at the airport were however occasionally reminded of Manston's dramatic past. The story goes that one day in more recent times, a controller asked a German pilot of an incoming passenger plane, 'Are you familiar with Manston?'

'No, but my father was in 1940,' the pilot replied.

Chapter 6

'One of the finest chaps that ever lived'

They shall grow not old, as we that are left grow old:
Age shall not weary them, nor the years condemn.
At the going down of the sun and in the morning,
We will remember them.

Laurence Binyon

The next phase of the Battle of Britain saw exhausted airmen and ground crews having to fight on day and night, while being continually bombed and strafed. Determined to gain control of the skies before invading Britain, Hitler had twice as many fighters as the RAF, and countless bombers. The fine spell of weather that had aided the Luftwaffe's final assault on Manston lasted around two weeks, supporting the Luftwaffe in their attempt to defeat the RAF. 600 Squadron were relocated to RAF Hornchurch near Romford in Essex where they stayed briefly before going on to RAF Red Hill in Surrey. With some of the coastal airfields now out of action, the Luftwaffe turned its attentions to the RAF bases in Greater London and to London itself. Once again, my father found himself at the heart of the action. But before long, as the dramatic days of August 1940 drew to a close, he had six days leave to do with as he pleased. Having been bombed within an inch of his life at Manston, it provided a welcome opportunity to head as far away as possible in search of a complete change of scenery.

He met Robby in London and they decided to take the train to Edinburgh. They had plenty to talk about while they waited for the train, recalling an evening they'd spent together a few days earlier. My father, Robby and Les Russell had gone into London to see Bing Crosby in *East Side of Heaven*. The air raid siren had sounded at 9.30pm and wailed for six hours. With no buses or tubes running, they had walked the streets of London until four in the morning. Chuckling at the unpredictability of their days and nights, my father told Robby that he'd spent a recent evening in Romford with a couple of Kiwi airmen. As was an almost daily occurrence now, the air raid siren had sounded that evening too and they had no option but to walk several miles back to camp while large fires burned nearby. My father yawned as more travellers joined them on the long platform. He had good reason to be tired having been out on patrol the previous night. 'Jerry was about all right, but darned if we could find him,' he told Robby.

On the way to Edinburgh, they had 'a heated argument with a couple of poms' about the RAF at Dunkirk. It helped pass the time until the train pulled into Edinburgh Railway Station at 6.00am. The two men began their time in Scotland by going straight to Edinburgh Castle. My father was especially impressed with Memorial Hall and the swords and armour. He and Robby made the most of every minute of their days exploring Edinburgh and rural Scotland. Dad's diary entries, particularly this one from the last day of their trip, leave no doubt about how much he 'liked the Scottish people' and relished his Scottish sojourn.

3 September 1940 – Today we toured Loch Lomond and the Trossachs. Loch Lomond is wonderful and is 22 miles long with the Highlands on either side covered with heather. It thrilled me to the core. Altogether we covered 210 miles of Scottish scenery today. Darn good. A fitting climax to leave.

In 2000, I did the same train journey from London to Edinburgh with my mother and father. We had a marvellous time looking out the window at the passing English countryside, telling stories and drinking cups of tea. I remember my 80-year-old father was in fine form, excited to be going on holiday to Scotland. Strangely, he never mentioned he had taken the same journey sixty years earlier. During our week in Scotland exploring far and wide, our most memorable day was touring Loch Lomond and the Trossachs National Park. My father absolutely revelled in the whole experience, quoting Scottish poets and regaling us with songs along the way. When I took my parents to the Edinburgh Tattoo set against the magnificent backdrop of Edinburgh Castle, dad never mentioned he'd been there before either, nor the following day when we toured the castle. I always laboured under the misapprehension that dad was only too happy to talk about his time during the war if you asked him. When anyone would say the men who had gone to war almost never spoke about it, I'd be quick to say, 'My dad is quite comfortable talking about it.'

I now know he only told us about the parts he was happy to recall; certainly not the gruesome details, or tales of death and destruction. He seemed to have been able to compartmentalise his memories, locking away the painful and traumatic ones, yet readily accessing events that recalled adventure and mateship. But why did he keep his memories of being on leave in Scotland locked away? I can only surmise that it had something to do with the fate of his best pal Robby with whom he shared his Scottish vacation in 1940. The war dealt harshly with many of the men my father sailed with on the *Akaroa* – including Robby. Nine were dead before their first Christmas in England. Robby would be killed ten months after their trip to Scotland.

In the blank memoranda pages near the beginning of his 1940 diary, my father kept a list entitled: *The missing, killed and wounded from our contingent of pilots, gunners and observers who left NZ 23rd March 1940. We honour them.* Included in the long list of names was Robby's, with a heartfelt note written beside it:

Sergeant Ivan Norton Robinson. One of my best pals and one of the finest chaps that ever lived. Survived a major crash in a Defiant just after we came to England. He was badly injured but made an excellent recovery and went back on Defiants. He was killed in a low flying accident on the 22nd of July 1941.

Tucked in my father's diary was a clipping of the memorial notices for his friend Robby:

Robinson – A tribute of love and remembrance to our only darling son and brother, Sergeant Ivan Norton Robinson, Royal Air Force, who lost his life July 22, 1941 as result of an aircraft accident overseas; aged 20 years.

> *If those lips could only speak.*
> *And those eyes could only see.*
> *And that beautiful picture was there in reality.*
> *Greater love hath no man than this.*
> *Inserted by his loving parents and sister Beverly.*

Ivan's death had a huge impact on his family and its thought his mother never got over his death. Of course millions of families around the world found themselves in the same heart-breaking position. Along with Ivan 'Robby' Robinson's family and friends, my father felt Robby's loss deeply. He and Robby had shared memorable times together: entering the RNZAF training school at Weraroa at the beginning of 1940, sailing to the United Kingdom, and exploring Scotland while on leave. Memories no doubt my father always treasured; memories that must have been too painful to share.

* * *

Heading back to RAF Hornchurch at the beginning of September 1940, my father was entering even more dangerous territory, as the Battle of Britain was about to intensify. By now, he had become so accustomed to the incessant singing of the air raid siren and the deafening barrage of bombs, that it didn't always keep him awake at night.

4 September 1940 – Left Edinburgh at 10.00am bound for London. Plenty of interesting scenery en-route. Arrived back at Hornchurch at 9.15pm to find parachute flares close to the drome and an air raid in progress. Not a soul about. Noise from bombs was terrific. Nevertheless I slept through it.

5 September 1940 – Large scale air raids again today. At about 16:00 hours enemy aircraft hit oil tanks on Thames Estuary. Large fires were started and in the evening clearly illuminated the sky. Visited Northolt drome and saw a Beaufighter. A hot job and armament includes four cannon firing forward.

6 September 1940 – Last night patrolled for 3 hours at 20,000 feet and just about froze. Received sad news of the death of Jack Brennan, one of the lads who came over with us. Spent last night on readiness. Bombs fell in my immediate vicinity.

7 September 1940 – Air raid all night long and am tired today. 500 enemy aircraft raided our area last night starting many fires. When darkness fell, whole of Southern England was ringed with large fires.

8 September 1940 – Readiness from Red Hill drome. One of the Blenheims got lost and crew bailed out. Machine crashed. Large number of enemy bombers over London last night.

9 September 1940 – Staying at Red Hill… Last night England appeared to be ringed with large fires. We may be staying here permanently. Went to bed at 9 o'clock. Slept the clock round. Have been given warning that the invasion is fairly certain to come this week. Many enemy aircraft over London today.

10 September 1940 – Arrived back in London area at Hornchurch. Spent most of night in air raid shelter. Once again many enemy aircraft over London. Fires were started in all directions. Anti-aircraft fire kept us up all night long. This in my opinion is showing poor results and affecting nerves as much as bombs.

11 September 1940 – Have been issued with service gas mask. At 16:00 hours, large formations of enemy aircraft flew overhead in direction of London. Left Hornchurch at 17:30. Went to Red Hill. Flew with our C.O. [Commanding Officer] *On readiness with Mr Pritchard, our Flight Commander.*

12 September 1940 – Last night I flew for just on 6 hours. At 23:45 landed at North Weald as we could not find our own base. Took off again at 03:00 hours. Saw two enemy aircraft illuminated by searchlights. We were a long way off and they disappeared before we got there. Watched dawn break.

The daylight bombing of London, the fourth phase of the Battle, reached a climax on Sunday 15 September when the Luftwaffe launched its largest attack against the capital. Around 1,500 aircraft took part in battles that raged until dusk. In Sir Winston Churchill's words, it was 'one of the decisive battles of the war.' *A day of rest, I don't think. Today 200 enemy aircraft were destroyed,* my father reported on this dramatic Sunday. Two hundred turned out to be an inflated figure. Reported information wasn't always reliable at the time. Nevertheless, the RAF had indeed thwarted the repeated attacks by the Luftwaffe that day. This crushing German defeat caused Hitler to postpone plans for invasion until further notice. It has frequently been said that without the bravery of the British airmen who fought in the Battle of Britain against such overwhelming odds, it is hard to see how the Second World War could have been won. The air battles on the 15 September 1940 became known as Battle of Britain Day.

After the dramatic daylight air battles that raged that day, my father was preparing as usual for night patrol: *On readiness tonight. Tons of archie going up.* Before they departed, two bombs fell about a mile from the aerodrome and demolished two houses. While on patrol that night, their Blenheim's wireless packed up. Several fruitless hours elapsed as they searched for the base while their fuel gauges crept lower and lower. All the while dreading the sound of engines spluttering out, they eventually managed to locate the airbase at 3.00am. My father was thankful it had been a moonlit night. He hadn't 'much fancied having to bail out.'

* * *

While stationed at RAF Red Hill in September 1940, my father acquired a bicycle. I know he was pretty chuffed with his new bike because he told me about it when I was growing up, one of the many stories that went towards painting an almost buoyant picture of his time in the Air Force. One day while he was tinkering with his new bike, a colleague, arriving back after spending the night in London, stopped to admire it. My father told him he had bought the bike at a shop in Red Hill for 25 shillings. While the two men looked the bike over, my father enquired about his colleague's night in London.

'It really took a hammering last night,' he said. 'People were walking about looking half dead this morning.' Feeling concerned about the intensity of raids on London, my father hopped on his bike; it was great to be on the saddle again. He hadn't ridden all year and it helped to take his mind off the difficulties they faced.

He reminisced about his more carefree days gone by, cycling in New Zealand with his mates.

A few days later, while he was having lunch in the mess, the men were suddenly called to immediate readiness. Sliding out of his chair, he left his half-eaten meal on the table and hastily dashed outside and mounted his bike. He began to pedal across the aerodrome towards the readiness point. Accompanied by a thundering roar, three Me 110s appeared in the skies above them. Craning his neck, he could see more detail than he cared to of the sleek and muscular fighters that were beginning to dive bomb the base. Filled with fear, my father found himself in the middle of the target area as bombs exploded around him. He pedalled furiously. Barely aware of his burning leg muscles, he zoomed on, dodging craters on the pockmarked field, as he frantically tried to reach the readiness point alive. Behind him, he heard an almighty explosion. Ground fire had brought down a Me 110 and it crashed dramatically near one of the hangars. The entire German crew were killed instantly.

Arriving at the readiness point he looked round, taking in the damage through the drifts of chalk dust rising from the pitted ground. The airfield was in bad shape. Numerous bomb craters dotted the grassy expanse. By evening, the ground had been repaired and the men were briefed for patrol. On the way to their aircraft, they had to drive past the crash site. Cranes had set to work to remove the wreckage of the downed Me 110. As they neared it, the dead bodies were all too apparent. My father looked away but the gruesome image of the German airmen's charred bodies was permanently imprinted in his mind. Traumatised, he climbed into their aircraft, desperately wanting to clear his mind of the awful scene.

Once airborne, another image soon replaced it as he surveyed the view below: fires burning right across the London area. The blazes were so extensive my father found it hard to believe that the city could survive. He knew the fires that raged below acted as beacons for the German bombers. High above London, he scanned the skies for enemy aircraft and, after a while, he spotted two. The pilot turned towards them. The chase was on. Once detected, the German planes didn't waste any time turning and heading for home. My father's Blenheim trailed them all the way to France but lost them somewhere over Europe. He was disappointed 'the bandits' had evaded them. The pilot flew them back to RAF Red Hill. Exhausted, they went straight to bed. But this eventful day hadn't quite finished. They hadn't long been in bed, when a 'dirty great bomb' fell nearby. Shaken, it was a while before anyone could fall asleep that night.

More aerial battles in the skies above Red Hill followed in the ensuing days. My father witnessed numerous dogfights. One day, while a great aerial battle was in progress, the all-clear sounded despite several enemy planes still wheeling overhead – someone had got their wires crossed. Several aircraft crashed in their vicinity. On 3 October, a Blenheim from 600 Squadron crashed in heavy rain in Sussex after an engagement with enemy aircraft, killing the entire crew. One of them was New Zealander Sergeant David Hughes who had only been with 600 Squadron for ten days. My father was very sad to lose 'Cobber Hughes.'

Another Kiwi, by the name of Pat Dyer, had also recently joined 600 Squadron. Pat, the son of the Paeroa police constable, got on particularly well with my father. Pat had done his training with the RNZAF at Weraroa and Ohakea on a subsequent intake, and then sailed to the United Kingdom on the RMS *Rangitata* in June. Like my father, he had been posted from RAF Uxbridge to the OTU at Aston Downs and then assigned to 600 Squadron. So far their journeys had followed the exact same path, and this pattern was set to continue.

One evening in early October, Pat and my father were chatting with a group of airmen at RAF Red Hill – *Sitting in mess after tea when (crump, crump!) one or two bombs fell on the drome. Jerry evidently saw our flare path.* More bombs followed. One incendiary bomb landed in the mess where my father had been sitting not long before. The fire was quickly put out. Fortunately that was the last time the men from 600 Squadron would have to endure the terror of bombs raining down on them in 1940. Soon after, it was announced that 600 Squadron were to relocate to RAF Catterick in Yorkshire to regroup and re-outfit with Beaufighters and the latest radar equipment. After more than three months on the heavily bombarded RAF bases of Manston, Hornchurch and Red Hill, life on the ground was about to become a bit less dangerous for my father, for a while anyway. I wonder if he breathed a sigh of relief as they headed north for the winter. Or had he not yet had his fill of 'red hot'?

Chapter 7

'Farewell to 1940 and all its troubles'

The fighters are our salvation but the bombers alone provide the means of victory.

Sir Winston Churchill

During the Battle of Britain, 600 Squadron were on night fighter duties. Although they were one of the first squadrons fitted with an early type of highly secret airborne radar, consisting of a screen calibrated to show the relative position of an enemy aircraft, it wasn't reliable enough to be particularly effective and night interception wasn't often achieved. My father reflected on his time during the battle later in life: 'We had very little success in tracking the German bombers even though we had the earliest form of radar,' he said. 'We would receive a blip signalling a German bomber, but at that time they were faster than us, and we had no chance of making contact. They would drop their bombs and then high tail it back to Europe.' No amount of effort could overcome the limitations of the early airborne equipment and for my father, life with 600 Squadron had often been more hazardous on the ground than it was in the air.

Now based at RAF Catterick, 600 Squadron were undertaking conversion training by day, and continuing their operational flights at night. There was plenty of extra company for the men at this airbase, with a Spitfire squadron having already withdrawn there, and two hundred members of the Women's Auxiliary Air Force (WAAF) also based at Catterick. Life seemed to ease up a little for my father during the remainder of 1940. Regular entries in his diary described enjoyable times. Rugby games were played with regularity. A group of New Zealanders formed the nucleus of the RAF Catterick rugby team and they did rather well, even defeating an Imperial Chemical Industries (ICI) team on one occasion. Entertainment Network Service Association (ENSA) concerts provided the men with light entertainment. My father marvelled at one particular concert soon after arriving at Catterick: *Concert on camp about the best I have seen on a RAF station. Good singing, beautiful girls, first class clown.* It was so good he went again the next night. The boys also enjoyed some of their free evenings in nearby Richmond. My father thought it was a very picturesque place with its cobblestone market square and ivy covered buildings. One especially merry evening, he and his mates won three statues in a shooting competition.

Along with the fun they had while based at Catterick, the men, of course, had in-depth training to undertake. They attended lectures on the theory of Air Intercept Radar and practiced using an Aldis lamp, a Morse code visual signalling device. It wasn't very often that the Luftwaffe flew nearby, but on occasion they were reminded of their more dramatic recent weeks. On the night of 20 October, bombs fell near the base. The next week, the region was hit again.

29 October 1940 – First frost of winter. Clean, fresh and crisp. Took off for some local flying with Sergeant Sansom. Lost aerodrome immediately in very thick haze. After tea everything was peaceful when up pipes the tannoy. Enemy aircraft in vicinity. Went outside and saw three Junkers 88 right overhead. They dropped their bombs on Leeming, 7 miles away.

During mid-November the Germans made a greater number of long-range night bomber sorties, than during any other week of the war.

Heavy attacks were made on Coventry, Birmingham and London. On 15 November, my father expressed concern: *Expecting Jerry to send over all his kites any night now.* Things remained tense the next day: *Quite a scare on at present. All aircrews are confined to camp.* That week they tested out a Blenheim with new engines. It had been fitted with a 9lb boost. During the test flight the speedometer touched 300 miles per hour. They also trained on new radar equipment in Beaufighters in the vicinity of Catterick Bridge. My father found it far more efficient than the version they had been using previously. With new aircraft and technology, 600 Squadron were being comprehensively prepared to re-join the southern airfields. Training by day, on readiness for patrol by night, the pattern of the days continued in this way. But with the arrival of winter, the weather would frequently curtail any night flying. Some days a thick frost covered everything, from the trees to the telephone wires, with a snow-white mantle. Unaccustomed to such a severe winter, my father was amazed when it would remain like that all day. With less and less flying, he and some of his colleagues were beginning to feel frustrated with the lack of action.

* * *

A few weeks before Christmas, my father went for a walk one evening with a couple of mates. On their way back they bought themselves a car. It was a spur of the moment thing. They split the £6 three ways and were now the proud owners of 'Susie' – an Austin 7. My father reported in his diary that she had a darn good engine and didn't seem to mind that the brakes didn't work properly or that they had to push start her. Susie helped to fill in the days ahead. Many hours were spent tinkering under the bonnet. They fixed up the headlamps and crank, replaced the oil, and put hooks on the bonnet. When they drove into Northallerton to try and tax and insure the car, none of the insurance companies would insure them, reportedly because they flew, but they did manage to obtain drivers' licenses. On the way back to the base they had the good and bad fortune to puncture right outside a garage.

One of the partner's in the car, Sergeant Rix or Ricky as he was known, had a crash one day and knocked a girl down. Fortunately she wasn't really hurt. Ricky was in more trouble for driving a car that wasn't taxed and so was summonsed to court. My father accompanied Ricky to Bedale police court and was relieved when the magistrate let him off with a £1 fine. After that my father persuaded a company to tax and insure Susie. Ricky must have decided that he and Susie weren't well matched because it wasn't long before he bought himself a Standard 8. My father, on the other hand, loved driving Susie and noted that she was 'going like a top.' Ricky didn't have much better luck with his next car. Given leave in the middle of December, he set off to go to Aberdeen in his Standard 8 with my father. Only six miles from camp, the car skidded off the road and wrapped itself around a lamppost. Fortunately both men were unhurt, but that was the end of their trip to Aberdeen.

Reading about Susie in my father's diary reminded me that his car was another detail, much like the bike, that he had readily shared. But he hadn't mentioned the car crashes or the trip to court. Had he simply forgotten those details or was I perhaps only given the half-full version of the memories he shared.

Having abandoned the trip to Aberdeen, my father chose to spend his leave in Exeter, relaxing at the home of his beloved war mother, Mrs Nicholls. He always enjoyed hearing about Mrs Nicholls life. Her late husband had been a judge, and they had spent many years living in India. Tragically, her son had been killed in the First World War, and her daughter now lived in New Zealand, so Mrs Nicholls was very glad to have 'her boys', as she liked to call the visiting Kiwi airmen, to look after. After several peaceful days off in Exeter, my father made his way back to RAF Catterick. En-route, he had a dramatic overnight stay in Blitz beleaguered London, a few days before Christmas.

22 December 1940 – Farewell to Exeter at 16:20. Train packed. Nursed a little child all the way to London. Arrived in the middle of the blitz. While trying to find King George Club, I got lost. No taxis running and not a soul about. Bombs falling and great flashes were lighting up the place. Eventually found it. Left London for York. Huge congestion on the train. Arrived back in camp at 17:00 hours.

* * *

Christmas Day for my father had always been the happiest of occasions, shared with his parents, grandparents, brothers and sisters on a warm summer's day in New Zealand. He loved singing carols while helping to shell the peas, and always hoped to find a sixpence in his grandmother's Christmas pudding. But on 25 December 1940, surrounded by snow in the heart of Yorkshire – with no family by his side, he struggled to believe it was actually Christmas Day. He couldn't help but be sadly disappointed when he didn't receive even a cable of greeting from home. Every effort was made, however, to make Christmas Day special for the servicemen at RAF Catterick. In the Sergeant's Mess, they dined on cream of tomato soup, roast turkey and sausage, roast goose and apple sauce, roast beef, baked and boiled potatoes, Brussels sprouts and mashed turnips. I know this because, tucked in dad's 1940 diary, I found a faded copy of the RAF Catterick Christmas Menu. On it, there are twenty-nine signatures. Some of the names I can decipher are J. I. Walker, A.V. Rix (Ricky), Lawson, A. Lipscombe, H.D.P.Dyer, A.V.Albertini, P.C.Whitwell, W.Ross, J.Wright. I feel incredibly honoured to hold the menu in my hand knowing that for some of these brave men, it was the last Christmas they ever got to celebrate.

For dessert, Christmas pudding with rum sauce was served, followed by mince pies, coffee, biscuits and cheese. All the Sergeants and Officers waited on the troops before serving themselves. Despite the fact they had dined so well, and the Luftwaffe had ceased its bombing raids on England for two whole days, my father didn't much rate his first Christmas away from home: *I can't really think it's Christmas day. Anyway, the worst I have had by far.* He brightened a little on Boxing Day when a letter and Christmas greetings from his mum arrived belatedly.

* * *

In the closing days of 1940, death featured heavily around my father. Pilot Officer Holmes died of his injuries after his Blenheim crashed into a hillside. My father was the leading pallbearer at the funeral. It was a new experience for him and he felt extremely sorry for the parents of his deceased friend. He also learned, with deep regret, that his Kiwi pal Alf Ritchie was missing. He would later learn that Alf's plane had crashed in Germany during an operation to Mannheim on the night of 22 December. By New Year's Eve, my father was in need of a few drinks to lighten the load.

31 December 1940 – Spent the evening with 6ft 3in giant Pat Dyer. Went to the dance and afterwards there was a party in the mess. Some of the Officers came, among them the new C.O., a Wing Commander. He was bald and Pat Dyer, in a very merry mood, tried to promote some growth by massage. This did not please the Wing Commander and he became very angry and immediately left the room. That was only one of many humorous episodes centring about old Pat. At 24:00 hours we all joined hands and welcomed in the New Year to the strains of Auld Lang Syne. Then began a series of scrums in the middle of the floor, with us New Zealanders taking a very prominent part. The party in the mess lasted until 05:00 hours, and so I close this year's diary. Farewell to 1940 and all its troubles.

It surely was a year of great changes for me.

Ian had begun 1940 as a butcher boy in Auckland. Now he was an RAF Air Gunner in the midst of a world war. It surely had been a year of great changes for him. But it was just as well he didn't have a crystal ball to know what lay ahead in 1941.

> *1 January 1941 – The dawn of a new year for me in England (Yorkshire) finds nature in a truly beautiful mood. Snow has fallen to a depth of six inches. The panorama of pure whiteness as far the eye can see amazes me as I stand and stare at the beauty everywhere. My car likewise is now white. Quite a lot of sore heads in the mess today. New Year's Eve was free of air raids. Drove the car down to the local village. Quite a thrill what with the blackout and drifts of snow to contend with.*

There's nothing like the dawn of a new year to provide hope and new resolve, as if the slate has been wiped clean and anything is possible again. Even though the world was at war, with no end in sight, the arrival of 1941 seemed to give my father a bit of a boost. But things got slower than ever in January as they waited out the severe Yorkshire winter. My father had already become frustrated with the lack of action in November and December. January only served to heighten his frustration. A group of New Zealand air gunners from 600 Squadron began to talk among themselves about what else they could do. They had come all the way from the other side of the world to play their part, but were feeling impatient and under-utilised. Until now they had been tasked with defending Britain under the control of RAF Fighter Command, but with winter slowing their efforts, they wondered if they might make a greater contribution by joining the bomber crews attacking Germany. After thoroughly discussing their options, several of them decided to apply for a transfer to RAF Bomber Command. Throughout January they waited to hear if their applications had been successful. The freezing conditions made working outdoors difficult. Some days everyone on the aerodrome would be needed to clear snow off the runway. The winter days dragged on with little to report.

20 January 1941 – Played billiards all morning. I'm fed up to the teeth with doing nothing. Wish I could get posted to bombers. Duty pilot all afternoon. No flying at all. Snowing fairly heavily. Excellent concert in the station tonight. Gainsborough girls were very nice dancers. Afterwards they came into the mess for half an hour. Don't look so nice off the stage.

A letter arrived from his mum that month bringing the sad news that his paternal grandfather had passed away in his eighty-ninth year. My father hadn't expected him to go so soon: *I should have thought he was good for 100.* Of course the tapestry of life at home went on unabated. People got married, babies were born, people died. Servicemen abroad had no alternative but to accept that they were unable to attend significant occasions. My father missed his beloved grandfather's funeral. That was just the way it had to be.

He spent a lot of his spare time that winter with his colleague Bob Landymore. Bob was married and had a cosy house nearby. Bob and his wife June often invited my father over. He liked Bob and June tremendously and greatly appreciated their hospitality. Dad kept in touch with them throughout his life, never forgetting their kindness or the camaraderie they shared during the war. I met June Landymore when she and my father were both in their eighties. She greeted my father like a long lost friend, calling him cobber the whole time we were together. I didn't glean all that many details from their memories of the war, but I sensed a special bond, borne, I guessed, out of experiences shared at this unique and challenging time.

By the end of January, with still no word about his application to Bomber Command, my father began to think seriously about applying to do a pilot's course. He visited the Education Officer and learned that the pilot's course had been condensed into twelve weeks. He immediately began swotting up on maths for the entrance exam. It was far better than doing nothing, he thought. I recognised this industrious and tenacious side to my father. He wouldn't have been happy sitting around twiddling his thumbs. 'If a job is worth doing, it's worth doing well,' he would often say, while applying himself to whatever task was at hand.

> *2 February 1941 – Snowing lightly this morning. Read the Sunday Pictorial News of the World, Sunday Graphic, Sunday Times and umpteen others. Swotted maths most of the afternoon. In the evening spent a couple of hours with Mr and Mrs Landymore and Curly Canham. Said goodbye to Curly as he has been posted to Whitleys. I'll probably see him again though. Maybe in a German Prison Camp.*

My father seemed by now to be anticipating a future stay in a German prison camp, only too well aware that was where bomber crewmen could end up. That is, of course, if they were lucky enough to survive. On 5 February, after attending a lecture on Morse Code, my father and five others, Pat Dyer, Tom Townshend, Peter Whitwell, William Willis and Fred Hindrup, received the welcome news that their postings to Bomber Command had finally come through. They were to go immediately to RAF Bassingbourn near Cambridge for training. My father packed up his things and got permission to travel to Bassingbourn by private car. He made sure Susie was ready for the 190 mile journey before saying his goodbyes to his colleagues. He was particularly sad to be parting ways with his dear friends Bob and June Landymore: *Damn fine pair they are too. Sorry to have to say goodbye to them.*

Once he'd completed his preparations for departure, he was about to go to bed when he unexpectedly received a telephone call from a senior member of the squadron. It was a pilot who he had often flown with.

'I'm ringing to see if you would consider staying on with 600 Squadron Ian? I'd hate to lose you,' the pilot said after apologising for calling so late.

My father glanced at his packed bags. 'I'm actually all packed and ready to leave for Bassingbourn first thing in the morning.'

'Yes, I thought you would be. But even at this late stage, I could arrange for you to stay on here.'

My father was flattered. He promised the pilot he would give the matter serious consideration overnight. He climbed into bed to mull over the pros and cons of staying versus going. After pondering the decision for a while, he closed his eyes and decided to sleep on it. The next morning, he woke with the certain feeling that he was making the right decision to transfer to Bomber Command, even though the odds of surviving were formidable. And so he bid farewell to Catterick and began the drive south. Dad once told me that not long after he left 600 Squadron, the pilot, who had tried to persuade him to stay, was killed in an accident in Southern England along with his new air gunner. With the benefit of hindsight, my father knew that staying in 600 Squadron would have likely been fatal.

* * *

Susie managed the long drive from Yorkshire to Hertfordshire wonderfully well. Flanked by snow-covered fields along the way, my father thought she'd driven like a thoroughbred. His mates were already there to meet him when he arrived at Number 11 OTU at RAF Bassingbourn. They had the weekend to settle in before the training course commenced.

Saturday, 8 February 1941 – Woke up in 'Herts,' RAF Bassingbourn. Went round and saw the C.G.I., a Squadron Leader. He told me that we are in number 27 course starting on Monday. The course will take about 2 months. The Sergeants Mess is very much overcrowded, meal times especially. Our billets are not much good. We have nowhere to keep our gear. Took Pat Dyer and Whitwell in to Cambridge in the Austin. Quite decent place. Went to the films. Saw Beau Vite win the Melbourne Cup. Arrived back in camp at 21:00 hours.

The following morning there was a mock gas attack using tear gas. The men were holed up for three hours in a 'rather smelly shelter' with about four inches of water in it. Once the course got underway, my father spent countless hours working with the Browning machine gun. He attended lectures on topics as diverse as armament, intelligence, Morse Code, and recognition of enemy aircraft. They even got the lowdown on being a prisoner of war. One day a Wing Commander gave them a lecture that my father described as a 'pep talk on Espirit de Corps.' They spent time on the range, practicing manipulating the Frazer-Nash turret, securing the Browning guns in position and firing rounds. My father thought the Wellington bomber's turret was slick, finding it worked on much the same principle as the Blenheim's turret he was accustomed to.

One day in mid-February, they paraded in honour of the New Zealand High Commissioner, Mr Jordan. Chatting with the Kiwis afterwards, Mr Jordan told them that he believed the food situation would be getting much worse in about a month. Grouped around the High Commissioner, they all smiled for a photo bound for the *Auckland Weekly News*. As Kiwis in RAF Bomber Command, they were among a truly cosmopolitan force. Many of the aircrew were from overseas, principally the Air Forces of Australia, Canada, South Africa and New Zealand.

* * *

Surprisingly, my father hadn't long begun his training at RAF Bassingbourn when he was allocated ten days leave. But it turned out to be fortuitous timing as he was about to celebrate a significant milestone. He drove some of the boys towards London, leaving his Austin in a garage on the outskirts of the city before taking the train to Liverpool Station. Strolling to the Victoria League Club, he was shocked to see so many burnt-out and blown-up buildings. The next morning, after bacon and eggs for breakfast at the Club, he caught the *Cornish Riviera* bound for Exeter. Lunch on board was a delicious affair – a far cry from what he was getting in the mess at Bassingbourn. He tucked into soup, stewed rabbit and roast potatoes followed by blackcurrant pie and custard. It was his twenty-first birthday and he must have decided to treat himself to the best available meal on board. Mrs Nicholls was pleased to see him when he arrived at her home that evening, but the next morning he realised his stay there would need to be cut short.

21 February 1941 – Sad news this morning. Mrs Nicholls can't get enough food in Exeter to feed us. The place is full of evacuees and they definitely can't feed any visitors. I am afraid I shall have to go back to London. Mrs Nicholls is not very well, confined to indoors now. Fading fast I think. She is heartbroken to think she can't have us down with her. Wonderful old lady.

Back in London, he took in the sights but had to spend several hours in air raid shelters each evening, awaiting the all-clear. He found it heart-breaking to see the people jammed together in the underground each night. The tubes had been fitted with wire sprung bunks in tiers of three. Only the children seemed to enjoy themselves down there, staying up late and having great fun playing on the escalators. One day he walked under Admiralty Arch from Charing Cross, then along Pall Mall continuing on up to Oxford Circus, viewing the damage all along the way. There were windows blown out of every second building. He strolled through the London Zoo but there weren't many animals left for him to view. He saw a burnt out monkey cage where an incendiary bomb had landed. Another day, he met a friendly policeman who gave him a bit of a tour. Having travelled all the way to Britain from New Zealand was a useful passport at times.

1 March 1941 – Shown around by a London policeman. Took me through several bombed areas where hundreds of people have been killed. £30,000 worth of damage done to the Ministry of Information. Went to a cinema. Saw 'Old Bill and Son.' Pretty nice picture. Took a tube back to Tottenham Court Rd. Air raid warning tonight. Tubes were crowded. Noticed five young chaps playing poker. Last night in London. All clear before midnight.

On his return to RAF Bassingbourn, my father had to hunt around for a bed. The camp had become even more crowded during his absence. He eventually located a spare bed in the drying room, before going to collect his mail. Tucked in a letter from his brother was a cutting from the *New Zealand Herald* reporting that 1,600 parcels, en-route from New Zealand to England, had ended up in 'Davy Jones Locker'. That explained why he hadn't received the parcel he had been expecting. It was most likely at the bottom of the sea.

The training course now included regular clay pigeon shooting on the range. He topped his group in an exam on the Browning gun and turrets, earning eighty-seven per cent. One free evening he went to a slide show and talk on New Zealand given by an English mountaineer. My father thought his collection of photographs was magnificent and felt proud to hear him say that New Zealand's scenery and climate were amongst the world's best. By the end of the presentation, he 'felt quite homesick for his New Zealand paradise.'

As the course progressed, the men were crewed-up and took to the skies to put theory into practice. Flying in a great Wellington bomber took some getting used to. It was nothing like today's experience of flying in a plane. Bomber crews had to contend with the constant deafening noise, numbing cold and continual vibration, all accompanied by a creaking, shaking turbulence. Landing the great bomber proved to be quite a challenge on one of their early training trips.

23 March 1941 – Snowing this morning. Lectured on theory of sighting. Cleaned four Brownings at No. 3 Nissen Hut along with Tom and Willis. After dinner weather cleared and I had my first trip in a Wellington. There was our crew of six and two instructors. Twas a cross-country trip. Base – Finningley – Cranwell – Ratcliffe – Base. Finished up bombing and air firing at Hatley Range. I fired 600 rounds then had stoppages in both guns. Terrific vibration of tail. Plane made me violently sick. The walk down the fuselage reminded me of walking over a rope swing bridge. Duration of flight, 3¾ hours.

27 March 1941 – On duty at 08:30 hours. Flying at 10:00 hours. Did an altitude and oxygen test cross-country to Andover, turned back at Worcester as weather was closing in. Up for 5 hours without any dinner. I was as hungry as hell. Flying above the clouds billowing out with peaks jutting up here and there, glistening in brilliant sunshine, was a truly wonderful sight. Sold the Austin today for £5. Sorry to part with it. A letter from mother today. Very welcome.

29 March 1941 – Overcast and cloud base very low. Took off at 11.00am on a two hour local trip. Flew around Cambridge at 500 ft. Then second pilot decided to land at Duxford. As he throttled back the throttle jammed and we rapidly lost height and were heading straight for a furrowed paddock. However the Captain made a gigantic effort and managed to open the throttle and we cleared the terra firma by about 10 ft. Our wireless device was carried away in the process. We all got a bit of a shock.

Pat had some New Zealand Anchor butter and biscuits sent to him. It tasted great.

On the next six-hour cross-country trip, he was relieved that they had been given rations this time. The sandwiches, chocolates and flask of coffee all went down well as they flew to the Isle of Man, spotting a Sunderland flying boat and a large convoy in the Irish Sea.

My father kept a keen eye on war developments: *The Jerry's have taken Salonika and also bombed Belgrade to ashes killing thousands. Hell! They call it civilisation*, he observed on 9 April. The following day he must have been mightily relieved he wasn't required on his pilot's training flight because the aircraft was shot down in flames by a Me 110 and crashed into a field. Thankfully the pilot escaped the burning plane with his life.

During an evening training flight on 16 April, my father noticed that London appeared to be getting heavily attacked. In fact, the city received one of its heaviest raids that evening, resulting in a record number of fires. Among the places hit was the King George and Queen Elizabeth Victoria League Club where he sometimes stayed: *One of the finest clubs of its kind. Many service chaps were killed. Hell I feel sore about that.*

During the final week of bomber training at RAF Bassingbourn, he was placed within a permanent crew. The six men were told that they would soon be joining 115 Squadron in Marham, Norfolk. There, they would begin the perilous business of night raids to Germany. During the new crew's first training flight together, my father was most impressed by the skill of his two pilots: Sergeant Sayers and Sergeant Tingley. As the course came to an end, my father had no regrets about leaving Bassingbourn, although he conceded the training they'd received had been exceptionally thorough. Since October, his life in the Air Force had been fairly undramatic, rather like the impression his stories had left me with. There had been a mixture of training and unremarkable patrols, peppered with sightseeing during periods of leave.

My father must have had an inkling that this was all about to change. But I wonder if he knew just how much more dangerous his work was about to get. The group of men who had transferred from 600 Squadron to the training unit together met in Royston for a final farewell. Having been posted to different squadrons across the country, the 'old gang' was about to be split up. As they bade each other farewell at the end of the evening, I wonder if they glanced around and wondered who among them would not survive the coming ordeal.

Chapter 8

'Hell, this is it'

If I should die, think only this of me:
That there's some corner of a foreign field
That is forever England. There shall be
In that rich earth a richer dust concealed;

Rupert Brooke

My father arrived at RAF Marham just in time for lunch. He'd thoroughly enjoyed the journey through the countryside from Hertsfordshire, where he'd undergone training for night bomber crews: *The fields and blossoms provided ample evidence of a real old English spring.* His new airbase, in the heart of rural Norfolk, was surrounded by flat, wide fields rolling gently towards the horizon. The heavy bomber station seemed almost at odds with its tranquil setting. Eyeing up his new base for the first time, my father thought it looked similar to some of the other RAF bases he'd seen over the past year. Stations that had resulted from the government's pre-war airbase expansion period typically had a lot in common. There were several standard RAF neo-Georgian buildings designed to blend in with the nearby country houses. An arc of five 'C' type hangars skirted the grass airfield, with a small, self-contained township tucked in behind. A group of brick and tile buildings housed a combined church and cinema, along with a fire station, sick quarters, shops and prison cells. My father was pleased to spot an exercise yard and playing fields next to the clutch of hangars.

Every effort had been made to disguise the airbase. All of the buildings sported a green and brown camouflage pattern. Lines of soot, designed to look like fences from the air, marked the large flying field. Exploring the station for the first time, my father thought it didn't seem too bad. The mess was first class, with two billiard tables and a ping-pong table. Best of all, he discovered that he could even buy chocolate at this aerodrome. Together with his friend Pat Dyer, who, happily, had also been posted to RAF Marham, my father spent the rest of the day settling in and meeting members of their new squadron.

It was only to be a brief acquaintance with some of his new colleagues however. Within days of his arrival, most of the squadron were detailed to go on a night raid to Brest. My father was not required for this particular operation and remained at the base. When he got up the next morning, he learned that several planes had run into serious trouble overnight. One crew had failed to return. Another had crash-landed. Yet another crew had bailed out, and a fourth plane had flown into a hill, killing the second pilot. My father was plunged straight into the harsh reality of life in Bomber Command where the likelihood of making it safely back from a raid was sobering.

He and his crew were dispatched to Boscombe Down to pick up the crew that had bailed out. As they made their runway approach for landing, he stared down at the colourful patchwork of farmland in the countryside below and could see that almost every type of plane had gone down nearby. He even spotted a Stratosphere Wellington. There was no ignoring the danger of flying in the RAF. It was on display right there in front of his eyes.

A couple of days later he awoke to the anticipation of his first night raid to Nazi Germany. He had been well prepared, but the enormous risk they faced was not lost on him. Opening his diary and noting the date, he silently wished his brother Keith a Happy Birthday. It was Anzac Day and this gave him pause to reflect.

25 April 1941 – Twenty-six years ago today the Anzacs were fighting for their lives. Today they are doing the same in approximately the same part of the world. The odds against them are terrific. But they fight with the same unconquerable spirit as their fathers did. We are going on operations tonight. Our first trip, they call it 'Freshman' trip! Made careful preparations, cleaned the guns. We have all made our wills etc. Going on a raid tonight. Taking 3000lbs of bombs with us.

Inspired by the Anzac spirit, as he contemplated his first bombing mission, my father needed to dig deep in search of his own unconquerable spirit. In all the stories dad told me of his time during the war, he never described the dangerous reality of being in a gun turret during a bombing raid. I remain in awe of anyone who would volunteer for this, and astounded that my humble father experienced these hazardous missions.

Wrapped myself up very well. Took off at 21:18. Circled the drome, dipped our wings in a farewell salute.

Arrived over the target about ½ hour after twelve. The kite wouldn't go any higher than 14,000 ft. Circled round getting shot at all the time. Searchlights tried to get us. Suddenly as we found the target, hundreds of searchlights and all hell of a barrage broke out all round us. The concussion of shells threw us about. 'Flaming onions' were curling over my turret in all colours of the rainbow. We were well and truly caught in a box barrage.

Hundreds and hundreds of shells came up at us. We were scared but bombed the target, which turned out to be Wilhelmshaven. By a miracle we got away and after losing our way and running out of petrol according to the gauges, we found Honington at 05:00 hours. I was worn out properly.

We had been flying for 9½ hours. Looking back it was like a ghastly nightmare. But it was a pretty good experience and at least we must

*have cost the huns thousands of pounds for that barrage. We couldn't
land at our own drome because it had been bombed while we were away.
I slept for about eight solid hours. Cleaned the guns today. Feeling
completely recovered and ready for anything else the ruddy hun has to
offer. The Anzacs are evacuating Greece. Hell I can't see the end of
this war for about three bloody years now.*

If my father had been under any illusion about the reality of a night
raid to Hitler's homeland, the extent of what he had taken on was now
only too apparent. I don't suppose anyone could ever be fully prepared
for their first bombing operation when the enemy is firing real live
shells. His vivid diary entry gave me the impression that he had found
the experience almost overwhelming at times. Although, having lived
to tell the tale, he was fired up and ready for whatever was to be served
up next. With his freshman trip under his belt, there would be even
more eventful trips to come. Like a recurring nightmare he would be
sent to face an uncertain future, night after night. His nerves and self-
control would be tested to the limit.

Having pieced my father's wartime journey together thus far, the
enormity of what he had been through was finally becoming very clear.
For the first time, I'm sorry to say, I realised just how terrifying it
must have been to be the lone rear gunner in a Wellington bomber,
dodging searchlights, flak and night fighters on a raid deep into the
heart of Nazi Germany. How gut-wrenching it must have been as his
mates were killed in action, one after another. My father had shown
incredible courage in the face of unimaginable horrors. Something I
had never really known, but something he could never forget.

Removed from the other crewmen, the rear gun turret of a bomber
was a lonely place. At the far end of the fuselage, the tail gunner
experienced the most extreme movements of the aircraft. My father
had worn three layers of clothing to try and keep warm. In the freezing
conditions, he had burnt his tongue on the thermos flask coffee that

had been provided for the trip. Strangely, it hadn't tasted all that hot up there. He made a mental note to drink his steaming coffee more carefully next time.

On his first operation the target had been the submarine and warship construction yards at Wilhelmshaven. My father's crew were one of eleven aircraft from 115 Squadron detailed to attack the German port that night. All eleven crews made it safely back. Captain Sergeant Sayers, my father's pilot, reported afterwards that they had dropped their bombs at 14,000 ft and observed bursts within the target area. Some pilots reported seeing large fires on arrival over the target. One crew saw their bombs burst between the armoury plant and the docks. Another was unable to locate the target and bombed searchlight concentrations instead.

Within days my father was preparing to set off on operation number two. During the morning, the crew flew a twenty-minute air test in their Wellington bomber. My father carefully recorded the details in his logbook, as he did with each test flight or operation. During lunch at the mess, they listened to a recorded dispatch of the evacuation of the Anzac troops from Greece. Later in the day the crew assembled in the briefing room. Unlike the mess where everyone often laughed and joked, here they wore deadly serious expressions. Talking was kept to a minimum. There was a large map of Europe on the wall. Each man took a seat and waited apprehensively for the words, 'Your target tonight is....'

Rotterdam was the target for my father and his crew on this particular occasion. The intelligence officers provided all the necessary information, showing them photos of the oil tanks they were to target. Anticipation enveloped the base as departure time neared. Airmen pulled on their fur-lined suits. Bombs were hoisted aboard each aircraft, guns were loaded and fuel tanks filled. Not long before the moment all their energies had been directed to, the operation was suddenly postponed. They needed to wait for the weather to improve.

Feeling impatient, my father poked through his rations for the trip: *An orange! Wonders will never cease.*

As midnight approached, they finally received clearance. A group of well-wishers were there to give the men the thumbs-up and send them on their way. The crewmen appreciated their support. My father especially liked their Wing Commander. He's a good old chap, he thought as he climbed into the plane: *Just like a father to us.*

My father hung his parachute on the hooks in the fuselage just outside the rear turret, since space was at a premium in the turret. The bomber's engine spluttered into life. Pilot Sergeant Sayers steered them toward the take-off point. When their turn came, their propellers began to scream and they accelerated down the runway, past the line of navigation lights, and lurched into the air. They climbed ponderously, passing over Norwich as they headed east towards the North Sea. Below, they could see several large fires burning fiercely.

Poor old Norwich getting blitzed, my father thought surveying the receding blazes.

Flying on through heavy cloud they reached 17,000 ft. Utterly alone over the North Sea, they were six young men in the prime of life, preparing to run the gauntlet of fighters and flak. In his own small world at the end of the dark fuselage, my father tested his weapons as the European coastline loomed. At the front of the aircraft, the pilots focussed on their instrument panel, bathed in a green phosphorescent light. In the cubicles behind them, the navigator manipulated his various aids, while the radio operator listened carefully for broadcast information. Even in the early stages of a raid, danger lurked. The airmen needed to keep a watch out for Luftwaffe fighters who might be stalking the English coast, hoping to attack Europe-bound bombers.

Once over Germany, they successfully located the target without incident and unloaded their bombs. The crew observed searchlights waving menacingly, trying to pick them up. Twice the searchlights beamed their bright cone of lights directly onto the plane. But happily, they remained unnoticed by the Germans below. My father was grateful for the plane's 'invisible' black paint that made them harder to detect against a night sky. Heavy flak thundered through the atmosphere, but it was well behind them and nowhere near their altitude.

After landing safely back in Marham at 04:00 hours, their next task was to debrief the Intelligence Officers. They, unlike the tired and hungry crewmen, seemed to be in no hurry to wrap up the meeting. Eventually the crew were released and headed straight to the mess to devour some ham and eggs for breakfast. Looking around at the other exhausted airmen in the mess, my father couldn't help but wonder who among the squadron wouldn't be coming back this time. Scarcely a night went by where at least one crew didn't make it back. Relieved to still be alive, he headed straight to bed after breakfast.

My father had survived his first two bombing operations. Reflecting on the month of April after some well-earned sleep, it was not lost on him that it had been a very big month:

A memorable month. Yugoslavia and Greece have been overwhelmed by Nazi hordes. Anzac forces fought a gallant fight, especially our Maoris who covered the retreat and evacuation. British & Empire forces together only numbered 60,000. In this epic action they killed and wounded 75,000 Huns for a loss of 3,000. In Libya our army has been pushed back to Egypt and are holding at bay a fierce German & Italian attack against Egypt and the Suez.

The battle of the Atlantic has taken a much more favourable disposition. The two German battle cruisers Scharnhorst and the Gneisenau have been put of out of action at Brest. This is a noteworthy achievement, as they would have been taking a heavy toll on our Atlantic shipping. Also the entire American Atlantic Fleet is patrolling half the Atlantic. Some German forces have landed in Greenland during the month.

I have done two raids (this week) and about 64 flying hours for the month. I believe that is my best. The weather has been good although it's a cold wind that blows across Norfolk. Have now completed 150 flying hours.

In between raids and air tests there was some down-time for the airmen. My father filled in time writing letters home and tumbling in the gym. On free evenings, the boys would head into town for a night out. They'd do some shopping, go to the pictures and enjoy a hearty meal at a hotel. It was great to get a decent feed and relax somewhat. Sometimes they could almost take their minds off the next raid. But my father's eventful third op would soon be upon him.

* * *

My father and his crew ascended into the night sky on 3 May 1941. The second of ten 115 Squadron aircraft to take off in quick succession, they were airborne at 21:19. Assailed by the noise of the engines, he looked back at the base pensively and wondered if he'd ever see it again. He wiggled his toes, trying to keep the blood flowing to his extremities. The bomb-laden aircraft hurtled onwards, piercing the darkness that enveloped them. At least it's a beautiful moonlit night, he thought, trying to stay calm as he stared into the vast, soothing emptiness, and admired the innumerable stars that pin-pricked the luminous dome above.

At every moment in the air, danger lurked. The gunner's task was to protect their aircraft from enemy fighter attack. Constant vigilance was required. What my father really needed were the eyes of a housefly so that he could simultaneously monitor the 360-degree spectrum. He scanned the skies continually for enemy night fighters who could obliterate them in a heartbeat. Cocooned in his perspex bubble at the tail-end of the monstrous bomber, my father plumbed the depths of his inner strength. He spotted another 'Wimpy', as the crews fondly called their Wellingtons, heading in the same direction. He tried to clear his mind of the men who hadn't made it back from operations, knowing full well that few airmen were ever pulled alive from crashed planes. He couldn't afford to think about how many men had already been lost. By the end of the war, over 55,000 Bomber Command aircrew would be killed. 20,000 of them were air gunners. And to my father, the dead were more than numbers on a page; some were friends and former crewmembers. It made no difference whether or not he was terrified of becoming another statistic. There was no option but to carry on.

That night the target was the Scharnhorst Battle Cruisers in Brest. As they arrived over Brest around midnight, the anti-aircraft fire was intense and got frighteningly close at times. They had some near misses as their bombs straddled the ship and docks below. Making a quick exit, the plane turned and headed for home. Twenty minutes into the homeward journey, my father could still see the large fire burning behind them in Brest. If the crew thought they could breathe a little easier as they left the German coast behind, they were wrong. Out of the blue, the plane's oil pump broke. They carried on nervously, flying over Britain's defensive moat, the North Sea. My father and his crew desperately hoped that they wouldn't find themselves at the bottom of the ocean as many doomed crews already had.

After what felt like an eternity, they passed over the waves lapping the English coastline below. They knew it wasn't uncommon for crews to run into problems in the later part of an operation when, having been in the air for hours, they were exhausted and cold. But they still felt relieved to be flying over home soil, and counted down the minutes until the dotted runway lights of RAF Marham appeared below. But their ordeal was not over yet.

Without warning, the propeller came off the starboard engine. It exploded and caught fire. Terror gripped the crew but automatic fire extinguishers quickly doused the fire. They knew they needed to try and keep clear heads, but adrenaline pulsed chaotically through their arteries. Having lost a propeller, they were lucky to still be alive.

Continuing on the port engine, they were slowly losing height. My father's heart pounded like never before. This was deadly serious. With some difficulty, they located an aerodrome at Oakington in Cambridgeshire and sent out a SOS. They waited.

There was no response. Then the remaining engine cut out. The pilot tried to restart it. My father tried to breathe but it was impossible to quell the rising panic. Their predicament was, quite clearly, a matter of life or death.

The pilot managed to get the port engine restarted. Everyone exhaled, releasing a fraction of the tension gripping their bodies. On they flew, all the while desperately waiting for a flare path to appear below. But there were still no lights to be seen. My father stared at the airbase beneath them, willing the flare path to materialise. Nothing but blackness stared back.

Then the engine cut out once more. Again they felt the dreadful sensation of quietly dropping lower and lower. The plane had restarted once but no one knew if the pilot could do it again as they descended, rapidly losing vital altitude. Everything seemed as if it was happening in slow motion.

There was great relief as the pilot managed to get the aircraft restarted for a second time. He had bought them some more time. But it was short-lived. Almost immediately the engine cut out again. No one dared to take a breath while the pilot frantically tried to restart it yet again.

With great effort, he got it going again. But now they were down to only about 500 ft. They sent out another SOS. There was still no response. And just when they thought the airfield below was never going to respond, the flare lights finally came on. They should have been bright beacons of light promising safety and a future. But it was too late. At exactly the same moment the flare path was lit, the engine cut out for the fourth and final time. The aircraft hurtled earthwards from 300 ft, the engine refusing to restart.

'Hell, this is it,' my father thought, deeply shocked at their predicament. Scarcely able to breath, he braced himself for all he was worth as they plummeted down from the sky, closer and closer to oblivion.

The earth rushed up towards them.

With a deafening graunch, the plane crashed into a poultry farm, throwing my father against the plane's framework on impact. His head smashed into a metal frame and he struggled with every fibre in his body to hold onto consciousness as the plane smashed uncontrollably through four henhouses, uprooting anything in its path and sending a riot of debris into the air.

As the indiscriminate trail of destruction slowed, the aircraft finally came to a stop.

Among the carnage, the plane lay in ruins, broken into two pieces. A deathly stillness followed.

Somehow my father managed to struggle out of the wreckage. He collapsed onto the ground. Badly shaken, he lay there for a few minutes with his heart thumping almost out of his chest, scarcely able to process what had just happened. It was 4.00am.

When he gathered his wits, he sat up and looked around to check on the rest of the crew. Except for the front gunner, who had concussion, they were all largely unscathed. Eyeing up the plane wreck, my father thought it was nothing short of a miracle that they had all got out alive. They had crashed only about half a mile away from the runway at Oakington.

Half an hour later, the ambulance from Oakington arrived to collect the six men: Sergeant Sayers, Sergeant Tingley, Sergeant Brittan, Sergeant Taylor, Sergeant Lambert and my father, Sergeant Walker. Stunned but alive, they were given a tot of rum and put to bed.

When dad spoke a little about this plane crash later in life, he left me with the impression that he was still quite astonished that it had actually happened to him. It seemed as though he was describing something that had happened to someone else. I suspect it had been an almost out of body experience to be in a plane that was tumbling out of the sky.

* * *

With a war on, there was no time to sit around and regroup. Surviving a plane crash was all par for the course. In fact one was considered lucky to be alive. And you were. It was straight back on the horse for my father's crew, flying to the RAF bases at Wyton and Harwell the next day. Back at Marham later that afternoon, he watched the Merlin powered Wimpy take off with a 4,000 lb bomb on board. With the perspective of someone who had just survived a plane crash, he looked beyond the base with new eyes. It was a lovely moonlit evening and he paused to savour 'the sweet scent of spring in the air'. He felt a profound sense of gratitude to be able to count himself among the living.

Back in his quarters he thought about his family in New Zealand. It was hard to be so far away from them at times like this. He reminisced about his happy, trouble-free life before the war and couldn't help but wonder if he would ever see his family again. He had survived one plane crash, but what were the odds of surviving another? He had recently written a letter to his parents to be sent in the event of his death. It had been tough to know exactly what to say. But a pamphlet he had acquired, entitled *An Airman's Letter to his Mother*, had got him underway. In a moment of vulnerability, he pulled out the letter from his locker, to reread what he had written. He felt grateful that his farewell letter had remained in his locker – so far at least.

Dearest Mother and Father,

Despite the fact that I feel no premonition at all, events are moving swiftly, and should I fail to return from one of the raids which fall to our lot in the very near future, I have asked that this farewell message be forwarded to you.

You can hope on for three or four months in case I am taken prisoner of war, but at the end of that time you must accept the fact that I have handed my task over to the very capable hands of my Royal Air Force Comrades as many other fine chaps have already done, including some third of the splendid chaps I came across with.

First it will comfort you to know that my task in this war as Sergeant Air Gunner has been of high importance.

For eight long months I have been engaged on twin engined night fighters, endeavouring to defend the cities of England...... Mother of the Free from German raiders.

Unfortunately the problem of defeating the night bomber remains unsolved and many towns in grim defiance display the mark of a fiendish foe.

During the 1940 September Crisis, I was stationed in the southeast part of Kent. The attacks on our drome were extremely violent and intense. I well remember one very warm ten minutes, at least 200 bombs fell all round us. For what seemed the longest fortnight of my life we were attacked on the same scale without respite. The Hun was a pretty poor shot, he probably only hit one building out of 200 bombs.

I have no doubt Jerry intended our base as one of his forward bases for his invasion. He would have got quite a shock had he tried.

It was then that I learnt through bitter experience the real meaning of war and the way the Hun wages it. As you know I have never born malice towards anyone, but my feelings for the Hun have been far from forgiving. I have never forgotten a direct hit on a shelter trench killing nearly 50 women of the Auxiliary Air Force.

For my part up till now I have been lucky, although I had some narrow shaves from bombs, life on night fighters was not very hazardous or eventful for that matter.

Some time ago I decided to join up with Bomber Command. My application went through and I am now on a heavy Wellington Bomber Squadron carrying out raids deep into the heart of Nazi Germany.

At this period, April 1941, we are fighting for our very life, in fact the British way of living: A measure of peace, freedom and justice. Something worth fighting for.

Although it will be difficult for you please at least try and accept the facts dispassionately for I shall have done my duty to the utmost of my ability. No man can do more and no one calling himself a man could do less.

How I have always admired your amazing courage Mother dear and your wonderful cheerfulness in the face of life's cruellest knocks, and how Dad always said 'When our ship comes sailing home!' It may be that some of the other boys will make the supreme sacrifice, I trust not.

At any rate my death... or even all your boys would not mean that your struggle has been in vain. Far from it, it means that your sacrifice is as great as ours.

Now I am trained to the mark, able and eager to throw my full weight into the scale against what is surely the greatest organised challenge to Christianity and civilization that the world has ever known. Thank you for that opportunity. I leave you to hold the fort after the war is won, as it assuredly shall be.

You must not grieve for me. I have no fear of death, just a queer elation. I would have it no other way.

In the immortal words of the poet: 'Somewhere on some foreign land there is a place that is forever New Zealand.'

Thus at my early age... God's will be done... my earthly mission has been fulfilled and I am prepared to die with just one regret and one only. That despite what I have written it will, I know, cause some pain and sorrow, but you and future generations will live in peace and security and I shall have directly contributed to that, so here again my

life will not have been in vain. Goodbye Mother and Father. I know I wasn't always good; but I wasn't bad.
                                        Your loving son

Goodbye and good luck Ray, Gladys, Keith, Lin, Cyril, Mary and darling little Betty.

He folded it back up and put it away, hoping upon hope that his Mother and Father would never receive this letter in their letterbox.

When I first came across his letter some seventy years after he had penned it, I was floored. It was shocking to think my father had stared death in the face at 21 years of age. And it wasn't just once. Time after time he came perilously close to losing his life. In the space of little more than a year, he had gone from being the young lad who wrote, 'Farewell Auckland, till we meet again' to a sombre Sergeant writing his farewell letter.

He sounded almost indifferent to the prospect of death. His one regret, the terrible grief he knew it would cause his parents. I wonder how dad's parents felt while their son was away at war? Had they wanted him to go? Did they dread receiving a letter like this? I do appreciate they were extraordinary times back then and can only guess they would have been proud of their son's courage and willingness to serve.

Bits of the letter hadn't entirely sounded like dad. I had never heard him say 'splendid chaps' or 'queer elation'. Still, I thought, times and people change. Until that was, I happened upon a website featuring *An Airman's Letter to his Mother*. Intriguingly, it contained some of the exact same sentences and paragraphs as my father's letter. I learned with further investigation that, in June 1940, *The Times* published a moving letter a mother had received after her son was killed in action. It was subsequently made into a short film, book and pamphlet, and widely distributed. At the time, the letter was published anonymously, but the author was later revealed to be Flying Officer Vivian Rosewarne, the co-pilot of a Vickers Wellington bomber who had also been stationed at RAF Marham. His aircraft was shot down in Belgium and the entire crew was killed. His station commander found the letter among the missing airman's personal possessions. It had been left open so it could be passed by the censor. The station commander was so moved by the letter that, with the mother's permission, he sent it to *The Times*.

I don't know if my father knew that the author of the published letter had, like him, been stationed at RAF Marham in a Wellington bomber squadron. If he did, I imagine he would have hoped that was where the similarities ended. A field in Belgium was not where he wanted to end up.

Chapter 9

'Another ruddy shaky do'

Courage is knowing what not to fear.

Plato

G etting back in a plane is one thing, going on a night raid after a plane crash must have been quite another. Three nights after they had crashed near Oakington, my father was scheduled on back-to-back raids. His fourth op was relatively uneventful. There was plenty of heavy anti-aircraft fire on their way to Brest, but it wasn't close enough to cause them any harm. He described the display of flaming onions as *just like a roman candle many many times exaggerated*. The pilot reported on their return that they had dropped one salvo of bombs heading southwest over the target, and seen them burst in the dock below. After some sleep during the day, the crew was straight back into it again the next evening.

8 May 1941 – Slept all morning. Got up feeling pretty tired to find that we are doing another for the second night in a row. Did an air test. Had tea and got briefed. Going to Hamburg. Took off at 22:15 with a big load of incendiaries. Passed over Heligoland. Searchlights caught us and heavy flak came very close. Terrific barrage over Hamburg. Dropped our bombs fair and square in the Blohm & Voss shipyards starting a large fire. Got back with 27 minutes petrol left. Another ruddy shaky do. We are all pretty nervous now after our crash.

My father was starting to feel the strain. It was hard not to feel dismayed that 115 Squadron was diminishing by the day. So many of his fellow airmen had not returned from raids and, for those that remained, it seemed as though it was just a matter of time until they too might not return. Of course the airmen had no way of knowing when their time would be up. Some men didn't survive their first raid; others carried on for months and sometimes even years. There was no logic to any of it. On a daily basis they had to deal with matters of life and death. Psychologically, it was a lot to try and cope with.

When I visited Marham decades later, I stared across the yellow rapeseed fields into the skies above the airbase. I tried to imagine the thundering Wellingtons returning from their raids at dawn, sporting bullet holes and damage that defied belief. I imagined the weary crews within, mightily relieved to have survived to live another day. I pictured the families in the nearby farmhouses, disturbed by the nightly rumble of bombers overhead. And I contemplated the airmen whose final steps on mother earth had been on this very ground as they walked towards their bombers, never to return.

My father had returned from his first five ops still in one piece. Having just worked back-to-back nights, he was shattered. Regardless, he decided to let off some steam with a group of mates going to King's Lynn for the evening. In town they went to the pictures and saw *Argentine*, before having a 'wizard' supper of eggs, steak, chips, peas, sausages, bread and butter. *There's certainly no shortage of food here*, my father observed knowing other parts of England weren't so fortunate. After a few drinks they headed home in the front gunner's car. The wireless operator sang to them all the way back. It was good to unwind a bit with the boys. Everyone was feeling the strain. Naturally they felt afraid at the height of an operation, not knowing if they would be alive the next minute. But no one said a word about it. Given the extreme danger they faced, many airmen must surely have been tormented by fear. But if they were, they typically kept it to themselves. The following day the entire squadron was on ops.

10 May 1941 – Maximum effort called for, about 400 bombers going over Germany tonight. Briefed for a trip to Hamburg again.

Took off in daylight. Target clearly visible. Intense anti-aircraft fire. Made a beautiful run over the target – Blohm & Voss shipyards. As we came out we were held in a searchlight cone of 16 searchlights. Dived down to six thousand feet but they held us for about five minutes. Thirty-three enemy aircraft were destroyed last night. On the way back, just off the Friscan Islands, a Me 109 tried to interfere with us, but after five minutes gave it up and we got safely back to base, landing in broad daylight.

He slept until 3.00pm the following afternoon before getting ready for the next raid. The large sign where he collected his parachute put a wry smile on his face. 'Each parachute has been checked by the Sergeant in charge. In case of failure please report.' Pre-operation preparations proceeded as usual. By now they knew the drill and simply got on with it. In their aircraft and almost set to go, the operation was suddenly cancelled. Deflated, they climbed back out and headed towards their quarters. At exactly the same time, undetected enemy aircraft were closing in on Norfolk. Only about a hundred miles away, Luftwaffe planes were making their final approach – and their target that evening was none other than RAF Marham. My father's operation may have been cancelled, but the men were about to see some action nonetheless.

May 11–12 1941 – Just after we returned, the Hun sorted out our drome and bombed hell out of us right up till 04:00 hours. Started a couple of fires and hit our mess. Plenty of cheek, he came down to 15,000 ft and could be plainly seen. A Ju 88. I'd much rather have gone on ops... There are a couple of unexploded bombs in the camp and a lot of the chaps have had to evacuate their billets. In daylight the poor old Sergeant's Mess certainly looks a mess. Lambert's car also caught a packet in the station garage… Our living quarters are very much overcrowded owing to extensive damage to the Sergeant's Mess.

My father had been stationed at RAF Marham for less than a month. It had clearly been a tumultuous time. He'd survived several raids to occupied Europe and walked away from a plane crash. But nothing was going to deter him, certainly not having the base bombed. That was nothing new. He knew there was no alternative but to get on with the task at hand. Danger, whether he liked it or not, went with the territory. At only 21 years of age, he'd already used up several of his nine lives, making the risks impossible to ignore. Fortunately, everything went fairly smoothly on the next op, soothing his frayed nerves somewhat.

16 May 1941 – Air test this morning for operations. At first doubtful, weather nearly had the whole show postponed. However they briefed us for a maximum effort and we are raiding Hanover tonight. Later on they changed the target to Koln. Rebriefed just before take off. Twas a real trouble free trip. Not a single gun opened up. Searchlights were ineffective. Target left in flames. Landed as dawn was breaking.

The squadron's Operational Record Book summarised this operation by saying: 'Although some haze over target, all crews claim to have identified the target and to have dropped their bombs on or close to the aiming point, starting a number of fires. All aircraft had returned safely to base after operations by 05:46 hours.' It had been a successful night.

* * *

In keeping with tradition, my father's parents had posted him the keys to the house for his twenty-first birthday earlier in the year. But with a war on, the parcel didn't arrive in Marham until May. He was delighted when he received it belatedly, and didn't seem to mind that it was nearly three months late. I was struck by the stark contrast to my life when I turned 21 nearly five decades later. I was living in a beautiful and safe country where freedom and democracy are prized, although I'm not sure I fully appreciated that at the time. Life was good. I certainly wasn't trying to save the world, unlike my father. Alone on the other side of the earth, without his lifelong friends and family around, he had to be content with a birthday card and a twenty-first key arriving by ship, three months late. A party would have to wait.

* * *

Arriving in London, courtesy of a week's leave, my father was shocked to see that only a couple of platforms remained at Kings Cross station. The station had received a direct hit during a recent bombing raid. He made his way out of the incapacitated station and headed to the home of a friend from 600 Squadron. Tommy Townshend's family gave him a warm welcome. Tommy and my father exchanged tales of their recent exploits. My father was interested to learn that Tommy had recently shot down a Me 110 near Hamburg.

Wandering around the West End, Tommy took him to see some of the buildings that lay in ruins. The restaurant where they lunched had no windows and hardly any roof left. The owner told them that they had been bombed three times, but he refused to be deterred. It was business as usual – well perhaps a little more al fresco than usual. Taking in a football game, my father was most impressed. More familiar with the game of rugby down under, it was something quite different for him: *Went and saw Arsenal play Tottenham Spurs. Soccer certainly is slick and the famous Arsenal were beaten three nil. Very big crowd in a grandstand capable of holding 90,000.*

While in London, he took the opportunity to visit New Zealand House and devoured all the latest *New Zealand Herald* newspapers. He learned his former 600 Squadron colleague Fred Hindrup, who he had trained with at Weraroa and Bassingbourn, had been posted as missing. My father would soon find out that, tragically, Fred had been killed in action during his tenth operational flight with his new bomber squadron. With so many of his mates being killed in action one after the other, my father may have started to fear reading the newspaper. It must have been hard to ignore the fact that if Fred Hindrup could get shot down soon after joining a bomber squadron, so could he.

London was stimulating, but what he really needed to unwind from his turbulent first month in Bomber Command was the sanctuary of his war mother's home. Conditions must have improved a little in Exeter and he couldn't get there soon enough. It was the next best thing to going home.

22–24 May 1941 – Caught the 'Cornish Riviera' to Exeter, a 4 hour journey. In a nice new train, easily the best I've been on in England. Some very pretty countryside. Rows and rows of tulips all different colours presented a wonderful sight. Arrived at the 'whare' at 15:00 hours. Mrs Nicholls is well and treats us like a mother…

Slept in till 9.30. The air in Exeter always makes me pretty sleepy. Went for a drive to Exmouth to see all the damage but to my amazement found very little at all. Strong fortifications all along the waterfront, rows of barbed wire entanglements and heavy guns in the hills behind. Devon is looking a veritable blaze of colour.

Slept in again… It's a real life of ease at the 'whare'. Did a spot of shopping and had a pukka haircut. Afterwards we had a drive through the lanes of Devonshire to see the cowslips, primroses and blue bells. Sat and talked to our 'War Mum' most of the evening.

* * *

Refreshed after a week's leave he expected to be straight back into action on his return to Marham. Instead a protracted spell of dismal weather slowed the RAF and the Luftwaffe. There was no option but to remain on the ground for the next fortnight. Despite the frustrating lack of action in the air, life wasn't exactly dull.

28 May 1941 – Cleaned the guns and turrets all afternoon. Briefed for a raid on Wilhelmshaven. Rebriefed at 20:00 hours for Kiel on the sister ship to the Bismarck. After we were dressed and in the kites the whole show was scrubbed. Johnny Brittan turned on supper with some food he had received from Canada.

29 May 1941 – No ops today. Dull and raining continuously. Did a spot of P.T. in the hangar. Situation in Crete is rapidly deteriorating although reinforcements have arrived. President Roosevelt's speech is almost undeclared war. The food in the mess about the worst I have struck yet.

30 May 1941 – Once again no ops tonight which makes it a whole fortnight since this place has operated… Went into Lynn for the evening. Saw 'Angels over Broadway.' Pretty corny. Scrumptious supper afterwards of ham and eggs. I seem to have been simply living on eggs lately. Haw Haw* gave it out that General Freyberg has been killed. Probably just lies.

31 May 1941 – Still no ops. Nothing important at all. Loafed around all day, playing cricket and tennis etc. Evacuation of Crete has started. Hell it's about time we had the Jerries evacuating… Last month has seen

---

* Haw Haw was the nickname given to the announcer on the English speaking propaganda radio programme, *Germany Calling*, broadcast by Nazi German radio to audiences in Great Britain and the United States with the objective of demoralising the Allies.

much activity in the air and on the sea. America seems nearer to active participation in this war. Two of the lads that were in my draft from New Zealand have received D.F.M's [Distinguished Flying Medal].

1 June 1941 – Most of the chaps were on church parade. But I was missed somehow. Anyway, I don't believe in being forced to go to church. No ops again. This has been an exceptionally bad spell of weather and neither air forces have been abroad very much.

2 June 1941 – Ops were detailed and our target was the sister ship to the Bismarck, Tirpitz, docked at Kiel. There were also two other cruisers there. However bad weather came up and the show was scrubbed. Anzac troops went through hell in and getting out of Crete. About 3,500 missing. From today, clothes in England can only be bought with coupons.

3 June 1941 – Sweet nothing doing… Our flight sergeant put twelve of us on a charge this morning for failing to fold up our beds. It's no wonder this war is being lost if there are chaps like him and the Wing Commander, who gave us ten days 'CC' [confined to camp], *at the head of things. Bloody petty little thing.*

4 June 1941 – Ops detailed once again on Kiel and once again scrubbed. Hell, what weather. Made up our ruddy beds. Blast them. Sad this squadron is getting like a training school. Think I'll try and get out East or anywhere out of this. Have been doing a fair amount of tumbling with Johnny Brittan, so am jolly stiff lately.

5 June 1941 – No ops detailed. Wing Commander called for volunteers to go to the Middle East. I jumped at the chance, so did two others of our crew… Received letter from Ray [eldest brother]. *He has been grabbed for overseas… Hope I go East.*

6 June 1941 – No ops again although they were detailed for Kiel. Bad weather is still predominant with much high convection cloud, which makes the danger of icing up highly probable. Still doing the confounded ten privileges and now have to report to the guardroom at 21:30 each evening.

7 June 1941 – Many Happy Returns to Mrs Nicholls. No ops tonight. Nothing doing all day. Dull and stormy.

8 June 1941 – Many many happy returns to mother. Hope she's not worrying about me. Still dirty weather and ops were curtailed once again. Our troops have invaded Syria and intend to forestall the Hun.

9 June 1941 – Weather is still in an ugly mood. Did a spot of P.T. and attended a very interesting and entertaining lecture all about the convoy system. The speaker was a Commodore and a real deep throated sea dog. His throaty chuckle greatly amused me. Johnny came back under the influence of whisky and caused a bit of a rumpus.

10 June 1941 – Very dirty weather and ops were detailed. We were briefed at 21:00 hours, the target–Brest.

After a month's respite, my father and his crew were finally given the go ahead to return to the night skies. Over the next four nights, he undertook his eighth, ninth and tenth bombing operations. The raid on the night of 12 June was the most fraught.

Nothing much was said as the crews prepared for departure. Sitting around for a fortnight, waiting for the gloomy weather to pass, had largely dulled conversation. Whatever thoughts they had, they pretty much kept to themselves. As the plane hurtled along the runway at take-off and staggered above the grass, my father had no way of knowing if he would ever touch the ground alive again.

Airborne thirty minutes shy of midnight, his crew was one of eighty-two aircraft Bomber Command sent to attack Hamm that night. Almost on cue, the moon came up. Approaching the European coast, the terrifying lights of the flak belt could be seen producing their incredible 'fireworks display'. But there was no going back. Happy Valley, as the crews called it, was the part of the trip they feared the most. Here they faced an almost overwhelming torrent of anti-aircraft fire heavily defending Germany's industrial stronghold, the Ruhr Valley. Once over Germany, their Wellington ran into frighteningly accurate and heavy flak streaming up towards them. It threw the plane about in an alarming manner. The acrid smell of cordite seeped into the aircraft. More flak hissed towards them, bursting into puffs sparkling with shrapnel, threatening the bomber's rugged fuselage. The geodetic basket-weave construction made the Wellington bomber unusually robust and able to survive damage that could ruin other aircraft, but this afforded little comfort in Happy Valley.

Dad later described how it felt flying over the Ruhr Valley during a raid. 'Sitting in the rear turret and watching the anti-aircraft fire coming up at us, I remember thinking it was rather like watching a glorified fireworks display,' he said. 'Everything seemed to be coming up in slow motion. The shells were bursting around us in black puffs, some close, some not so close, and it was rather like being observers of a really special display on Guy Fawkes Night.' He painted the picture of a surreal world. It was as if his mind had struggled to process what was actually going on at times.

Lumbering on towards the target, they navigated the dangerous Ruhr Valley. Minutes and hours ticked by as they passed over the rivers and railway lines that weaved beneath. Eventually they dropped their bombs among the guns and searchlights in the position they believed to be Hamm. But in the haze, no results were observed. After leaving their heavy calling cards, they turned for home. But two German planes were suddenly on their tail: a Me 110 and a Ju 88. Typically the return journey was the more dangerous one because on the way to the target, the Germans didn't necessarily know where a plane was going. But once it had turned for home they knew exactly where it was going; they knew it was trying to get back to England. Some smart action by pilot Sergeant Sayers saw them evade the enemy aircraft. But it wasn't long until one of their engines failed. Flying on nervously, they finally sighted the English Coast and knew RAF Marham wasn't far away. They were mightily relieved when they landed at 4:32am, exhausted but safe.

The crew had come to thoroughly rely on their captain, Sergeant Sayers. He had led them through ten successful raids and they trusted his skill implicitly. When my father learned that Sayers was being posted to the training unit at RAF Lichfield, he was 'very sorry to be losing him.' In fact, it turned out to be rather a sad week. Death was hovering even closer than usual. As well as bidding farewell to his trusted pilot, one of the 'civvies' working in the mess, who my father thought was a particularly nice chap, was killed when nearby King's Lynn was bombed. Four enemy aircraft were destroyed during the raid and my father witnessed one of them coming down in flames.

Then, one of the crews from his squadron crashed during an afternoon air test. The aircraft caught fire and all six crewmembers were killed. Among them was Sergeant Hart whose bed, in their sleeping quarters, was right next to my father's. I imagine he would have been feeling rather emotional when he wrote in his diary: *Shocking affair! He was getting married on his next leave.*

Later that evening they were set to depart for a raid to Dusseldorf, but when the wireless operator turned on the wireless, it blew a valve; they were delayed until it was fixed. Eventually taking off at eleven minutes past midnight, they discovered that the aircraft wouldn't go any higher than 700 ft. With their engines overheating, they had no option but to return immediately. They knew only too well that bringing the aircraft back down with a full bomb load on board could be catastrophic. However the new pilot managed to make a 'super' landing, seventeen minutes after take-off. My father reported that he had noticed 'a few Jerries snooping about' during their brief time in the air.

A few days later, a number of crews were detailed for a raid to Kiel. At the last minute, his crew discovered that their airspeed indicator wouldn't work. It was the third time in a row they were scrubbed as a result of technical problems. The following morning he learned that two planes had failed to return from Kiel. My father had known one of the missing pilots ever since they'd joined the RNZAF together. Filled with sadness he penned: *Jillett is a fine chap and I'm very sorry.* Sadly Sergeant Jillett's aircraft had been last heard from at 3.35am calling for assistance. They had crashed into the sea sixty miles from the enemy coast, killing the entire crew. One after the other, the losses around my father were mounting. As well as coping with the grief associated with each loss, he was confronted with the very real fear that he could be next. But fate had another plan, for this month anyway.

* * *

During the last week of June 1941, my father was sent on a weeklong refresher course to Newmarket. Accompanied by his mate, Pat Dyer, and the front gunner from his crew, Ted Lambert, he found the practice invaluable and enjoyed getting to see a little of Newmarket. He kept a particularly close eye on war developments, with Germany having just begun its invasion of the Soviet Union.

Sunday 22 June 1941 – Germany is marching against Russia without giving any warning at all. This Hitler bloke is certainly a bit of a lad. The whole world has been at war in the past two years now. Flew to Newmarket today. Our course starts tomorrow morning. We are billeted right in Newmarket in the 'Cottage'. Newmarket is quite a pleasant spot and the weather is really beautiful, almost a heat wave. Our mess is in the grandstand of Newmarket racecourse, the orderly room in this place is in the tote house and the Armoury backs onto the stables. Makes a fine aerodrome though.

Monday – We got cracking straight away and went out off the coast doing air to sea practice. I did pretty well at that. Practice in identification and range judging. Cleaned the guns. Had an early night so went to the pictures in the fair town of Newmarket... Russians claim to have destroyed 98 German aircraft yesterday.

Tuesday – Cine camera gun practice all morning with fighter affiliation of Hurricanes. Very good practice. Hurrys are hot stuff. Had lunch. Went air firing – air-to-air drogue target. I did best out of our bunch with 10 and 12 holes respectively. Excellent practice. Heat is still terrific. Duke of Kent and the A.O.C. No 3 Group visiting us tomorrow. Finished work about 9 o'clock. Felt tired out. The Russians have lost three towns including Brest Litovsk. Claim to have destroyed 58 enemy aircraft.

Wednesday – Lecture about Russia in general and Russian aircraft by C.O. this morning. Air to ground firing at Me 110s cut out in the ground. Good fun. Later cine film show and the visitors royal. All had our picture taken with H.R.H. Duke of Kent. Must try and get one. Air-to-air drogue firing and air to sea. I didn't do so well air to air. Think I was allowing too much deflection. Must do better tomorrow.

Thursday – Weather as hot as blazes. Cine camera gun work this morning with Tomahawk affiliation. They don't appear as good as Hurricanes. Air-to-air in the afternoon. Shot both drogues away... Saw a film of our fighter attacks. Mine was quite good.

Friday – More fighter affiliation with air to air again. Pat Dyer did very well. Spent the afternoon .22 shooting ordinary and snap. I did best with snap scoring 42 out of 50. On the clay pigeon I topped the score with 9 out of 10. Also did a little out of the turret. Pretty hard. Finished off with range judging and identification. Strolled around Newmarket and retired early. Russians still doing well.

Saturday – Made out my logbook. Have done 18 hours flying here… In a final pep talk the C.O. told us to kill as many Jerries as we can – it's the only medicine they understand. Returned to Marham at 15:30.

Having appreciated the change of scenery in Newmarket and the opportunity to hone his skills, my father had been blissfully unaware of what had been going on back at the base.

Chapter 10

'Rabbits'

In thought, faith,
In word, wisdom,
In deed, courage,
In life, service.

Anon
(Written in my father's diary)

A rriving back at RAF Marham, my father was keen to find out how everyone had been getting on during his week away. He greeted the first airman he saw.

'What's all the news around here?'

The smile disappeared from the airman's face. 'You haven't heard then?'

'Heard what?'

'About your crew?'

'No. What's happened?'

'Well, it's… it's bad news I'm afraid. Your crew went on a raid to Cologne just after you'd left. They crashed at Debach [Suffolk] on the way back.'

'*Crashed*?'

'Yes, I'm afraid so.

My father was shocked.

'And ah… Fred Tingley was killed.'

My father's heart sank. Fred was their second pilot and he liked him very much. 'What about the others?' he said, trying to stem the emotion welling up inside him.

'They're badly injured I'm afraid. Broken legs, fractured sculls.'

My father could hardly believe it. He began to walk away, dismay and disbelief among the emotions he was struggling to contain. It was extraordinary timing. If he hadn't been sent away for training, he would have been on that fatal trip. Was it just pure chance that he wasn't on the plane? Or was it good luck, his double crown perhaps lucky after all? Perhaps it was providence – the hand of fate or destiny? By an unfathomable miracle, my father-to-be continued to survive the war, against the greatest of odds. Many airmen must surely have pondered the mysteries of life and death. One RAF pilot[*] wrote: 'Death was always present, and we knew it for what it was. If we had to die we would be alone, smashed to pieces, burnt alive, or drowned. Some strange protecting veil kept the nightmare thought from our minds…' Given the numerous times my father cheated death during the war, it almost seemed as if he had a 'protective veil' cast over him.

Feeling 'cut up' about his crew, my father didn't seem to mind when the Gunnery Leader decided, at the last minute, that he would replace him on that evening's raid to Bremen. Having caught a cold, my father was 'feeling rotten' and was grateful to be able to get an early night. Feeling a little better the next morning, the returned crews told him about the overnight attack at breakfast. Three crews from the squadron had failed to return and were now officially 'missing in action'. Those who had made it back told him that it had been almost as bright as day during the raid, with the northern lights illuminating everything. Nearly everyone reported having seen enemy fighter planes during the trip.

---

[*] RAF Pilot, Group Captain Peter Townsend: Philip Kaplan, *Fighter Aces of the RAF in the Battle of Britain* (Great Britain: Pen & Sword Aviation, 2007), p. 159.

He took himself off to a quiet spot to write in his diary. As had become his habit at the end of each month, he reflected on what the month of June had brought:

An historic month sees Germany at Russia's throat and Britain promising aid to Russia which Stalin has gratefully accepted. A British military mission has already arrived in Russia. Significant fact that the Germans are not bombing Moscow, evidently afraid of Berlin getting it as well. Our aircraft losses have been very heavy this month.

* * *

With most of his old crew still wounded, my father was allocated four new crewmembers. Pleased to still be with his friend, front gunner Ted Lambert, my father was surprised to discover his new pilot, Flight Lieutenant Litchfield, was a fellow New Zealander who hailed from New Plymouth, not far from Koru. The new team was scheduled on four ops over eight consecutive days.

6 July 1941 – Attended a pleasant church parade with the station band in full accord. Have had my NZ tabs sewn on at long last so I was in all my finery. Met our new Captain, Fl/Lt Litchfield.

7–8 July 1941 – Gloriously fine. There were ops last night to Munster, which must be taking quite a pounding. Very little defence there. Hardly any flak. Litchfield has decided to go on ops to Munster tonight. The only opposition is likely to be fighters.
*   Took off into a clear full moon. We found our target and dropped our eggs on the railway station. There were many large fires and the Ruhr Valley seemed to be one mass of fires. The only opposition we encountered was the 20 mile zone of searchlights. These are very*

effective. Arrived back at 04:00 hours. Spent most of the day trying to sleep through very humid weather conditions. Did not sleep well. Went into the ancient town of Lynn. Met our Captain and the Gunnery Leader. Fish supper in some dingy restaurant.

9–10 July 1941 – Got up at my usual late hour after a non-operational night – 08:45 hours. Attended a 10 minute prayer meeting which the padre has inaugurated to be held once a week... Did an air test. Briefed at 20:00 hours. Target is Osnabruck in northwest Germany. Plenty of flak and searchlights are reported...

Experienced considerable opposition getting through the famous searchlight belt. Picked out on four occasions but quickly out. The target was easily identified under a moon-drenched sky. The flak was accurate. I saw two other Wimpys over the area. Coming back the dikes in Holland were sharply defined and were rather interesting. We were diverted owing to fog and landed at Upper Heyford, which has a rotten mess. One of our crews bailed out through petrol shortage. Waited around all morning to be interrogated with twenty-six Hampden crews. Returned to base at 15:20. Retired worn out at 18:30 hours. Slept for fourteen hours without a break.

11 July 1941 – Exceptional weather conditions still prevail. Did an air test for ops. Briefed at 20:00 hours. Wilhelmshaven is the target. Lots of flak and searchlights. Also tonight is my 13th trip. Had a letter from Buck.

Ops were cancelled at 22:15 owing to bad weather, so I still haven't done the jinx trip.

13–14 July 1941 – Ops tonight. Cleaned the guns and harmonised two kites... The raid is on Bremen with 114 aircraft on the target. So I do my 13th trip on the 13th.

Duly took off at 23:00 hours. Developed engine trouble just after crossing the German coast. Turned back and bombed the night fighter aerodrome at Borkum Island. Encountered no flak and searchlights. The engine was red hot all the way back and we had some anxious moments. But got safely back. Slept all day.

None of the five 115 Squadron crews in action the following evening found the trip to Duisburg plain sailing. One crew returned to base early, reporting engine trouble. A second returned having experienced intercommunication problems. Another crew failed to return at all. One of the pilots who made it to Germany and back reported that it had been impossible to locate the exact target in such heavy cloud conditions. My father's captain informed his squadron leaders that they had dropped their bombs from 13,000 ft in an area east of Duisburg owing to violent enemy opposition. They returned having sustained flak damage to the aircraft's nose and tail. My father seemed rattled by the experience.

15–16 July 1941 – The target tonight is Duisburg in the Ruhr Valley. We have a strange aircraft, which I don't like very much.

Last night's trip was bloody hot. The flak kept bursting all round us – so close that we could hear and feel the concussion of them. Their deep searchlight belt took some getting through. I was shaken up all night. After landing about 4.30 this morning we found six holes in the aircraft. One just missed the pilot.

Pat Dyer is missing. After all these months we've been together, makes me wonder when my turn will come. Damned hard luck. Still maybe he landed up in a prison camp.

Reading that Pat Dyer had failed to return, I knew my father would have been mightily upset as he penned those words. Dad had mentioned him so often in his diary and they were clearly firm friends. His Kiwi companion seemed to be the one constant during these turbulent times. They had been together in 600 Squadron during the Battle of Britain, and had transferred at the same time to bombers, both ending up at RAF Marham. Now Pat was missing, my father wasn't ready to accept that his friend might be dead. He dearly hoped Pat might have survived the crash and become a prisoner of war. That was the best of a bad bunch of possibilities for those who hadn't returned. Throughout the war, family and friends of each lost airman often had agonising weeks and months to wait before their fate was confirmed. Most would eventually be listed as 'missing believed dead.' My father wouldn't learn Pat's fate for quite some time. Sadly, any hopes he held for Pat Dyer were in vain. He was in fact killed in action that night. Along with my father's crew, his was one of thirty-eight Wellingtons sent to attack Duisburg. On the way to the target, Pat's aircraft was attacked by a German night fighter and crashed near Roggel. There were no survivors. Henry David Patrick Dyer was 22. He is buried in the Netherlands.

When I first read my father's diary entry that Pat Dyer was missing and learnt, with the click of a mouse, courtesy of the New Zealand War Graves Project, that he had died that night, I burst into tears, emotion overwhelming me. I felt surprised by the force of my reaction, but still the tears came. Here was a man I had never known, who had died over seventy years ago, but the tragedy of it hit me like never before. He was my father's mate, and he was gone. I felt a profound sense of loss. I'm not entirely sure why. Perhaps I cried the tears my father never could. He had to remain strong. He had to climb back into a plane. He had to continue to fight for a better world for the children he may never have. And to my father, it was now no longer a matter of *if* his time would come, but when.

* * *

Pat Dyer's loss prompts the memory of a day I shared with my father in September 2005. In a black cab in London, we were on our way to Westminster Abbey on Battle of Britain Sunday, for the sixty-fifth anniversary service. I'd helped dad pin his war medals on his jacket and he looked just the part. It was an important day for which we had travelled a long way.

'How are you feeling?' I asked him, as the cabbie navigated Piccadilly Circus.

'A bit emotional,' dad said, turning to look out the window.

It wasn't like my father to admit to being emotional. He wasn't one to even talk about emotions. I was surprised.

He was momentarily lost in reverie. Then he looked back at me and smiled faintly. 'I'm just remembering all my friends who didn't survive the war,' he said blinking. 'So many never lived to see this day.'

I was surprised to hear him say this. I'd never heard him talk about any friends who died during the war. But then again, I shouldn't have been surprised. Tens of millions of people didn't survive the war. We carried on in silence for a while. I had that nagging feeling that there was a lot I didn't understand about my father's wartime experiences. But the moment quickly passed, distracted by the famous London landmarks we were whizzing past like counters on a Monopoly board. When I think back to that conversation, I am now much better placed to comprehend my father's feelings that day. Having since discovered so much more about his day-to-day life during the war, I'm not at all surprised he was feeling emotional. I imagine he may also have been contemplating the injustice of it all. Why had he survived when so many had fallen? Why had he been chosen as one of the lucky ones, honoured at a special ceremony decades later, while others had crashed unceremoniously to their death on a foreign field?

* * *

Back in July 1941, my father was due some leave having worked solidly for more than six weeks. He and a friend decided to take advantage of the fine summer weather and took the train to Bournemouth. As the English countryside whizzed past, fellow travellers offered them sandwiches, cakes, chocolates, cigarettes and books, keen to express the gratitude they felt towards those in the service. My father appreciated how kind everyone was as they journeyed to the seaside.

Smelling the sea air on arrival at Bournemouth, he wasted no time escaping to the beach. The long pier stretched into the English Channel like a bridge to nowhere. Quaint and colourful beach huts added to the charm of the long, sandy expanse. With the sand trickling through his toes and the sun warming his head, he paused to experience a rare moment of pure contentment. Even if bustling Bournemouth was a far cry from the rugged, untamed beaches he was more at home with in New Zealand, there was nothing quite like a day at the beach for this island boy.

20 July 1941 – Went down on the Bournemouth sands. The beach was teeming with people. Sea beautifully calm and warm sunshine. Had a dip. Water was fine. Great place this Bournemouth. Full of huge hotels and cinemas, flash restaurants etc. Lots of New Zealanders about that have just arrived in England. I met a chap named Young that used to ride for the Whangarei Cycle Club... Talked for hours with some of the others. Mushroom omelette for supper.

After savouring the sea and sunshine at Bournemouth, he headed to London, towards the end of his week's leave, to enjoy a couple of days there. I suppose the knowledge that he would be off to bomb Germany again within days was always in the back of his mind. Or perhaps he preferred to try not to worry about future events that he couldn't prevent from happening anyway. By pure chance, my father ran into his good friend Les Russell in London. He and Les talked until 2.00am.

Comparing notes, they discovered they were both feeling 'pretty fed up.' My father was interested to learn that Les had destroyed a Me 110 during an intruder patrol to Lille a couple of months earlier. The two men met up again the next morning at the Lyons Corner House in the Strand. They continued their catch-up over a salad and coffee before taking the tube to Waterloo. Here they parted, each one returning to their respective squadrons.

My father never saw Les again. While Les would survive a crash-landing near Oakington in March 1942, he wouldn't be so lucky two months later. He was killed when his Halifax crashed during a raid to Germany. Flight Sergeant Leslie Plimmer Russell was originally buried in the Central Cemetery in Mannheim and later reinterred at Durnbach War Cemetery in Germany. Les, like so very many, gave his life during the war, in the service of humanity, that others might be free. I never knew my father's friends who made the ultimate sacrifice, but I will always remember them.

* * *

Having returned from his week of leave, my father expected to be straight back into ops, but bad weather prevented any flying for several days. He became increasingly frustrated by the lack of action.

> *29 July 1941 – Still dirty weather. Ops were detailed for Brest but later scrubbed… They announced over the tannoy that ops were cancelled. Most of the blokes cheered. Maybe they will realise one day that the quicker Germany is bombed the sooner the whole blasted affair will be over.*

Despite the bad weather, the airmen put their time on the ground to good use. My father attended a lecture on escaping from a German Prisoner of War Camp. He found it 'exceedingly interesting' and reported that

Angela Walker, Anzac Day 1975. Photo: *The New Zealand Herald*/newspix.co.nz

Crossing the equator on the SS *Akaroa*, April 1940.

Air Gunner's Course, Weraroa, January 1940. Ian Walker, front row, third from right. He wrote on the back of this photo: "only 4 came back."

SS *Akaroa* approaching Panama, April 1940.

No. 27 Course for Wellington Bomber Crews, 11 OTU, RAF Bassingbourn.

Sergeant Ian Walker and Sergeant Patrick Dyer at RAF Bassingbourn.

Sergeant Leslie Plimmer Russell. "The one and only," written on the back of the photo.

Warrant Officer James Ian Bradley Walker. Sir George Grey Special Collections, Auckland Libraries, AWNS-19410827-26-6.

Visiting Kloster Haina, formerly Stalag IX A/H, in 2014.

Josephine Nicholls.

Angela Walker at Sergeant Ivan Norton Robinson's grave, Byley, Cheshire.

German – Allied Prisoner Exchange, Barcelona, October 1943. Photograph taken by Pérez de Rozas. Arxiu Fotogràfic de Barcelona.

New Zealand protected military personnel repatriated from Germany move along the quay at Alexandria – Photograph taken by George Robert Bull (1910–1996). Ref: DA-03216-F. Alexander Turnbull Library, Wellington, New Zealand.

Above: New Zealand repatriated prisoners of war entrained on Alexandria wharf for Maadi, Second World War – Photograph taken by George Robert Bull (1910–1996). Ref: DA-03217-F. Alexander Turnbull Library, Wellington, New Zealand.

Right: Alex Templer-Feeney and Sachin James Subramaniam, grandchildren of 1943 repatriates Gaythorne Templer and Ian Walker, commemorating Remembrance Day 2014.

Ian Walker talking with HRH Prince Philip, the Duke of Edinburgh.

Ian Walker admiring the Battle of Britain Monument, London 2005.

Ian Walker finding his name at the Battle of Britain Monument in London in 2005.

Ian Walker signing autographs after the unveiling of the Battle of Britain Monument, London 2005.

Angela Walker finding her father's name at the Battle of Britain Memorial at Capel-le-Ferne.

he had learnt a great deal. I suppose it would have been impossible to ignore the likelihood that he could end up in a POW Camp, if he survived at all that was. Yet another month had passed by. On the eve of August 1941, he once again reflected on war developments:

Another month that will go down in the martial history of the world. July has seen Russia do what no other country has done and that is 'stop' the Nazi hordes. It has been estimated that 1000 Nazi soldiers, sailors and airmen have been killed and wounded on the Russian front. Japan appears to be on the verge of war with us. American aid is reaching gigantic proportions. From now on Berlin will be razed to the ground. R.A.F. is powerful enough to do it now.

Having survived over three months in bombers, my father knew he was going to need all the luck in the world to make it four. As soon as he woke up on Friday 1 August, he made a point of saying 'rabbits' out loud. It was a superstition he had grown up with. The idea was that you would receive a month of luck if the first word out of your mouth, on the first day of the month, was 'rabbits'. I well remember when I was growing up dad would creep into my room on the first morning of the month and mouth as quickly as he could, 'say rabbits'. He would be delighted if I did and seemed almost convinced of the power of it. Perhaps his experiences in August 1941 had given him good reason to believe in it. He had even written 'Rabbits' at the top of the page in his diary on the first day of August. Curiously, it was the only month he ever wrote this in his 1941 diary. Perhaps he knew, at some inexplicable level, that this month he was going to need all the luck in the world, and then some. He was probably also aware that Germany had been dramatically strengthening her air defences. There were now many more defensive fighters for the allied crews to contend with over Europe. So many, in fact, that in the first eighteen nights of August 1941, 107 British aircraft were lost.

August hadn't long begun when my father's crew were detailed for what would be his fifteenth op. The odds of surviving this many operations were heavily stacked against an airman. A great many bomber crews got shot down after only a few trips. Remarkably, you stood a greater chance of surviving as an Infantry Officer in the First World War than you did completing a tour of thirty operations with Bomber Command. My father returned safely from his fifteenth op, describing it in his diary as usual. Some of his colleagues weren't so lucky during the raid, and my father had the shocking misfortune to witness the moment a nearby crew were blasted to eternity.

3–4 August 1940 – Our target tonight is Hanover. A real town blitz – with the post office as the objective. Took off into a thick fog and dirty weather. The weather was lousy for our little jaunt to Hanover. No searchlight opposition due to 10/10 cloud. There was plenty of flak but it was not very accurate. Passing Bremen I saw an aircraft receive a direct hit from flak. It was a ghostly sight – a huge flash then a ball of flame hurtled earthwards. Coming back we got lost and finished up with a wireless fix in the middle of the North Sea. Landed at an aerodrome near Hull at 06:00 hours after having been in the air for nine and a half hours. I was pretty tired and glad to get to bed.

That was the last time that my father made an entry in his red, pocket-sized 1941 diary. The pages from 5 August to 31 December all remain ominously blank. The diaries of the 55,000 men in Bomber Command who died during the Second World War must also have ended abruptly one day, blank pages the only thing remaining. Chills ran down my spine when I first saw all the blank pages in my father's 1941 diary. Even though I already knew what had taken place to prevent him from writing anything further, it made what followed seem all the more real – and all the more shocking.

* * *

On 5 August, my father and his crew set off into the night skies at 10.47pm in their Wellington bomber, serial number R1471. With half a tour under his belt, this was his sixteenth flight towards Nazi occupied Europe. He had complete trust in the other members of his crew: their Captain – Flight Lieutenant Frederick Lorne Litchfield, Second Pilot – Sergeant Richard Hammer Hilton–Jones, Navigator – Sergeant Donald Arthur Boutle, Wireless Operator – Sergeant Alexander Scott Lawson, and Front Gunner – Sergeant Edward ('Ted') Frank Lambert. Their lives were quite literally dependent on the vigilance and skill of each other. Alone in the sky, they were six men against the Reich.

The sun had already set in the west as they flew in near darkness towards the German coastline that night. They looked forward to seeing it rising in the east on their return. Flying over Germany, one of their engines began to give them some trouble. Despite this, they continued on towards their target. But it wasn't long before the pilot became sufficiently concerned that he announced they should jettison their bombs and head back as fast as possible. They chose a nearby bridge and rapidly unloaded their bombs.

As they were turning for home, they were caught in a searchlight cone. With no associated anti-aircraft fire they had good reason to be worried. Searchlights without associated flak meant there were certain to be German night fighters about. The pilot immediately took violent evasive action. Diving and turning to the left and right, the bomber hurtled through the air in a complex corkscrew manoeuvre. But the highly skilled German searchlight operators were able to keep the illuminated aircraft firmly stuck in their cone of light. The pilot put the plane into another deep stomach-churning dive and this time, though not without considerable difficulty, managed to escape the searchlights.

No sooner had the men breathed a sigh of relief than a German fighter, flown by Lieutenant Hans-Joachim Redlich, seemed to appear out of nowhere. Now flying on only one engine, the Wellington crew knew they were in serious trouble. To add to their woes, my father discovered the hydraulic system that operated his turret wasn't working. The engine that had failed controlled this system. He was faced with a fighter right on his tail and no guns at his disposal. Rendered defenceless, he knew it would take only one on-target shell to vaporise them.

The enemy fighter unleashed a burst of gunfire. The bullets whizzed towards them. Fortunately they were slightly off target. My father's highly skilled pilot took further evasive action trying to shake off their attacker. By nothing short of a miracle, he managed to evade the fighter. But by now, and with only one engine working, they had lost considerable height and were down to about 2,000 ft.

With the fighter off their tail, my father tried to breathe deeply in an attempt to calm his harried nerves. Everything seemed relatively okay. He knew the Wellington bomber was quite capable of flying on only one engine. Despite the gnawing apprehension deep within him, he tried not to let doubt infiltrate his mind. Getting back safely was all he needed to focus on.

On they flew. But it wasn't long before he heard front gunner Ted Lambert suddenly scream out.

'Let me out, open the door,' he cried, sounding highly agitated.

My father's heart began to pound. He had no idea what the problem was up the front, but things didn't sound at all good.

'Let me out, let me out,' Ted screamed again, this time even more urgently.

It was obvious that Ted desperately wanted someone to open his door. The bulkhead door behind his front turret could only be opened by the pilots on the other side. My father listened for the pilot.

Nobody responded. The lack of response gave him further cause for concern. He sucked in sharply, looking below as he tried to gauge their altitude. The pitch darkness encompassing the enemy territory below stared back at him, providing no clues as to its depth. From the rear turret, he didn't know exactly what was going on in the rest of the aircraft.

'What's the trouble Ted?' my father said through the intercom, although, from his position in the rear, completely isolated from the rest of the crew, there was precious little he could do.

Silence

He listened again. Still no one said a word. He tried to ignore the suppressed fear building inside. But it was impossible. Something must be very wrong. He looked anxiously out into the endless blackness all around him. But there were no clues as to the nature of their predicament.

All of a sudden, with no warning whatsoever, there was a thundering, almighty graunch. The plane was careering through tall trees and into a potato field. With no idea of their position, my father was horribly surprised by the deafening 'rending crunch on impact with mother earth' in the fleeting moments before he passed out. Complete blackness followed as he lost consciousness.

In the wee small hours of the morning in the nearby village of Glabbeek, the commotion startled some of the local Belgians. They jumped out of bed.

Regaining consciousness in due course, my father tried to exit the wreckage. If he was injured, he didn't know it. He managed to open the turret door manually.

Dropping a large distance to the ground, and a lot further than he'd anticipated, he felt a shattering pain in his leg, so intense, he passed out again. Shattered bones protruded through the flesh below his knee.

Astonishingly, Ted Lambert's front turret had been knocked off the aircraft on impact and had rolled around and around eventually coming to rest. Ted, who miraculously emerged with scarcely a scratch, dashed over to check on the others.

The rest of the aeroplane had splintered into two pieces, each half ending up about 50 ft apart. Pieces of wreckage were strewn chaotically amongst broken branches and scattered leaves.

My father drifted in and out of consciousness. Ted and the two pilots, who were also largely unharmed, dragged the injured crewmembers away from the aircraft, over to the edge of a clearing. It was pitch black and they could hardly see a thing. The pilot explained that tall trees had broken their fall. Without trees to cushion their impact, it is unlikely any of them would have survived the crash. (Perhaps this was the genesis of my father's deep-seated love of trees.) Sergeant Boutle was in the worst shape. He had sustained a fractured skull. Sergeant 'Jock' Lawson had an injury to his face. The pilots went back to the aircraft and, as they had been trained to do, set fire to it by exploding the oxygen bottles. Nearby, villagers spotted the fire and rushed out to help. The crewmen heard them coming but didn't recognise the language they were speaking, though they sounded friendly enough. The airmen asked the villagers where they were and learned that they had arrived, unannounced, in the middle of Belgium.

Their rescuers helped them back to the village, carrying the injured men on stretchers. It was a five minute walk to the home of Franz and Bertha Willems-Harry on Kersbeekstraat in Glabbeek – Zuurbemde, and they ushered the airmen inside, along with next-door neighbour Mr de Becker and mayor Victor Mertens. Bertha cut Sergeant Donald Boutle's parachute off him as he lay on a stretcher, to ease his laboured breathing. Local doctor, Dr Homans, gave my father some medication for the pain emanating from his left leg. Everyone was most concerned about Donald who, apart from being helped to sit up to vomit, lay motionless on a mattress with his eyes closed. His face was swollen and covered in blood. Mr de Becker could see that the other airmen were young and handsome, but couldn't tell if Donald was a man of 25 or 55. He was in such a bad way that it didn't look as if he was going to survive. None of the locals spoke English but the airmen managed to make themselves understood when they asked if there was a priest nearby. Pastor Van Maegdenbergh arrived with holy oil and administered last rites.

As morning approached, Franz and Bertha gave the men some breakfast. My father felt ever so grateful for the kind way they willingly shared what little they had and hungrily devoured his food. Mr de Becker was amazed at my father's appetite despite his badly fractured leg. Word of the airmen's presence soon spread and most of the village filed in to see their 'RAF heroes'.

With three of the crew badly injured, the villagers had no option but to notify their German occupiers in order to arrange for an ambulance to take them to the nearest hospital, in Leuven. With a compound fracture of the leg, my father was about to officially become a prisoner of war. But he was alive. He breathed a huge sigh of relief. Not just because he had survived the crash, but also because the horror of night raids to Germany was finally over. Having left England abruptly in the dead of night, he realised that, ironically, crashing into a field in Belgium had just preserved his life, releasing him from further perilous bombing raids.

Now however, instead of being in a plane that dropped the bombs, he was on the very ground that would be subjected to heavy bombardment for the next few years. But he didn't concern himself with that right now. He just felt a strange sense of relief. Having already survived something akin to Russian roulette, he certainly had good reason to be relieved. The work he had been doing was so hazardous that, in 1941, more RAF aircrew were lost over Germany than German civilians killed on the ground.

I'll always remember how palpable dad's relief still seemed when he told us about surviving his plane crash in Belgium. He hadn't known how he could have endured the horror of night raids indefinitely, yet carrying on had seemed his only option. I always marvelled at this man who, despite being bound for a prisoner of war camp with shattered bones to boot, seemed to have been profoundly grateful to have arrived on a foreign field, alive. Whatever was to follow, my father couldn't even begin to imagine.

Chapter 11

'Darkness always gives way to light'

The sun with loving light makes bright for me each day, the soul with spirit power gives strength unto my limbs.

Rudolf Steiner

My father opened his eyes and looked around the small room he was in. He recognised Donald and Jock lying in the other two beds, surrounded by hospital paraphernalia. Aware of a dull ache in his left leg, he looked down the bed and saw it had been placed in traction. The image of the plane crash flashed into his mind, and then everything came flooding back. He recalled the sickening thud as the plane had unexpectedly careered into the ground. He'd had no idea the aircraft was going to crash, and didn't know exactly what had caused it. He remembered floating in an out of consciousness before being looked after by the kind villagers. The Germans had arrived with an ambulance. Now he was in hospital. He turned his head and gazed out the barred windows. Nuns were tending to a vegetable garden in the hospital quadrangle below.

A nun in nurse's uniform appeared by his bedside. She radiated a kindness that he hadn't felt for awhile. Miraculously she spoke English. Smiling, she patted his arm reassuringly, and told him the doctor would see him soon. In due course a doctor entered the room and made his way over to examine my father's leg. He thought the doctor seemed a particularly kindly man and felt relieved that everyone so far seemed to be so compassionate. The Austrian doctor smiled at him.

'Ich bin nicht ein Nazi,' he said quietly.

My father nodded and smiled back at him. He realised the doctor was trying to tell him that he wasn't a Nazi. That explained why he was receiving such good care. With his leg so badly injured, it occurred to him that his dream of one day achieving international cycling success could be in jeopardy. But for now, there were more pressing challenges to focus on. What was to become of him? Unable to walk, an enemy in Nazi occupied Europe, he didn't like to think too hard about what may lie ahead. In a hospital room in Belgium, with a shattered tibia and fibula, his immediate future didn't seem bright.

Things were even worse for Donald in the bed beside him. At least he was still alive, though he remained unconscious for nearly two weeks. Jock was recovering well, and was sent on to Germany after a few days. His bed was soon occupied by a Frenchman recovering from the removal of an explosive bullet from his buttocks. He'd been shot while trying to escape. They were three injured men locked in a room, but the passing of the days and weeks were eased by the extraordinary kindness of the Franciscan Sisters who helped to make their circumstances more bearable.

Dad wrote about the Sisters in a letter many years later:

As I lay there on my back, life seemed dark and grim. But darkness always gives way to light and it came in the form of these angels of mercy–the Sisters from the convent, who every chance they got would surreptitiously pass me the most wonderful goodies, cakes and sweets.

One day a Sister who spoke English hurried over to his bedside when no one else was around. This particular nurse often took the time to talk with him and knew how upset he was that his parents back in

New Zealand would know by now that he was 'missing in action', but wouldn't know that he was very much alive. It broke his heart to think how worried they must be. The Sister had good news.

'If you'd like to write a letter to your parents, I know someone who is going to England. They can post it from there for you,' she told him.

My father thanked her profusely, feeling greatly relieved at the prospect of his parents learning that he was still alive. The Sister smuggled him in a pen and some paper and he immediately began to write a letter. He begged his parents not to worry about him, explaining that he was being well looked after. His family had been made aware that he had failed to return from an operation, within days of the crash. His friends back home and the cycling community soon learned that he was 'missing in action' while reading their local newspaper.

Missing on Operations–Well known Amateur Cyclist

One of Auckland's best known amateur cyclists and holder of many trophies, Sergeant James Ian Bradley Walker, has been reported missing on air operations. He is the fourth son of Mr and Mrs W F Walker of 31 Malvern Rd, Morningside.

Born 21 years ago in New Plymouth, Sergeant Walker was educated at Mount Albert primary school and Kowhai Junior High School. He was employed by R and W Hellaby and Son, Limited, before enlisting with the Air Force at the outbreak of war. After being trained at Levin and Ohakea he proceeded overseas in March of last year.

During his school days, Sergeant Walker was a most promising Rugby footballer and was a member of the Kowhai team which won the Auckland Rugby Union's primary schools championship in 1931. Later he joined the Eden club but eventually gave up football in favour of cycling.

As a member of the Manukau Amateur Cycling Club he won the 25 miles junior championship in 1937, the 42 miles senior harbour race in 1938 and the 100 miles race from Papakura to Ngaruawahia and back in 1939.

Years later his mother showed him the letter he had written to her from his hospital bed in Leuven. Incredibly, it had reached her, bringing the wonderful news that he was alive. Not that she had doubted it. From the moment she had been notified that her son's plane had failed to return, she had believed wholeheartedly that he was alive. Somehow – call it mother's intuition – she just knew. But the letter, confirming her deep conviction that he was alive, brought enormous relief to the whole family.

My father had never felt as grateful to anyone for anything as he did to the Sisters who provided the means for him to communicate with his family, risking their own lives in the process. He never knew exactly how the letter had got to New Zealand, but based on what he learned after the war, he wondered if the person who took the letter from Belgium to England had been an intelligence agent who operated on a Lysander aircraft. Dad found it remarkable that his letter had been successfully smuggled out of Belgium so early in the war.

He had also written a letter to Donald Boutle's parents from his hospital bed and they received it, five months later, in January 1942. It turned out that it had arrived via Sergeant Jack Newton, the first British airman to evade capture and return to England, after being helped by members of the resistance along the Comete Escape Line. In an extraordinary coincidence, Sergeant Newton had been in a Wellington bomber that had crash landed in Belgium on the same night as my father and his crew. One of the many people who helped Sergeant Newton along the way was a nun whose house he stayed at in Brussels in August 1941. This nun worked several days a week at a nunnery nearby. I wonder if she had been in contact with the nun who helped my father, and that was perhaps how Sergeant Newton came to have the letters.

Flat on his back in his hospital in Leuven, with nothing much else to do but think, my father wondered what had happened to the uninjured members of his crew. He hadn't seen them since that fateful night in Glabbeek and had no way of knowing where they were. He wondered if they had been able to escape before the Germans arrived. Lying there, he imagined them on the run heading for freedom in Switzerland. But his hopes were in vain. All of his fellow crewmembers ended up in POW camps where they remained until the end of the war.

I don't suppose he thought too much about the German fighter pilot who he had almost been able to eyeball shortly before their crash. Without the luxury of the Internet at his fingertips, dad never knew that the name of the pilot who claimed the combat victory in bringing down their Wellington bomber, was Lieutenant Hans-Joachim Redlich. According to the records, their aircraft crashed at 2.34am, 3 kilometres from North Tirlemont. Redlich was a member of the Luftwaffe night fighter wing 1 – NJG 1 based in St Trond. My father's aircraft wasn't the only plane Redlich was credited with shooting down that night. Forty minutes later he downed a Halifax. Unbeknown to my father, another RAF crew were struggling out of their wreckage about 20 kilometres away from Glabbeek, near St Truiden. One of the crewmembers lucky enough to survive was Australian Flight Lieutenant Thomas Barker Leigh. Tragically, he wouldn't be so lucky in 1944 when he was one of the fifty recaptured men shot after 'The Great Escape'. Luftwaffe pilot Redlich was himself killed, only a few months after attacking my father's aircraft, during a practice flight in January 1942. He is buried in Lommel, Belgium.

* * *

While in hospital in Leuven, my father was chuffed when a nun gave him a book to read. I remember him telling me that he had read this book, *The Seven Silver Sisters*, some seven times. Often, during the afternoon, music of the great composers would waft from the convent into his hospital room while he read. He though the nuns played their beautifully toned piano with great feeling. This part of his odyssey was a time dad seemed to enjoy reminiscing about. I heard about the nuns and the book they gave him to read, several times. Bookended by challenging chapters, his time in Leuven seemed to have been a peaceful interlude, somewhat removed from the rigours of war. He felt tremendous gratitude for the skill and kindness of his Austrian doctor who had strung his leg up with an ingenious system of wires, wheels and weights in order to pull the bones out again into a position where the leg could be put in plaster. It took about three weeks to stretch the bones out to the necessary position. My father always said that this doctor couldn't have treated him any better, even if he had been his own son. Dad's profound gratitude to his doctor and to the Sisters who cared for him, never left him. His gratitude was such that he hoped to be able to go back and thank them one day. It would be a dream that quietly burned within him for decades.

* * *

My father couldn't stay cocooned within the convent hospital indefinitely, and was told after nearly seven weeks in Leuven that he would be moving that afternoon. And so began a series of stays in different places during his incarceration in Nazi occupied Europe. The next stop was Institut Bordet in Brussels, where he was placed in a ward with about a dozen other injured Royal Air Force prisoners. Fellow patients had extraordinary tales to share. They too had emerged alive from the wreckage of their bombers, against the odds, or bailed out into the pitch darkness above Belgium.

A doctor at this hospital re-examined my father's left leg. It hadn't healed at all well. The doctor told him there wasn't much sign that the bones were knitting together as they should be, and placed his leg back in plaster. My father was surprised how well the doctors and nurses treated them. At this hospital in Brussels, the Allied airmen were treated with just the same high level of care as the local patients. The fact that they were meant to be enemies didn't seem to enter into it, dad told us years later, still amazed by the humanity displayed. Once again, the kindness of the nurses had touched him deeply.

One particular German nurse took a liking to him. Knowing that he would soon be bound for a POW Camp in Germany, she made it her mission to teach him some German. In the box of mementoes my father kept from his wartime days, I discovered a small brown notebook that he had acquired during this time. The notebook came from Papeterie Robert in Brussels. Perhaps his friendly German-speaking nurse had given it to him. On the first twenty-five pages he had compiled his own 'Deutsch–English Worterbuch.' His self-made dictionary begins with 'der mann – the man, der frau – the woman' and carries on page after page until it concludes with a final, perhaps hopeful entry, 'gnade – grace'. Clearly the nurse had taken a lot of time sitting with him as they compiled this lengthy list. I had always been surprised how much German my father had picked up during his time in Germany. Now I realise that, thanks to this unofficial tuition, he had a smattering of the language before he even arrived.

* * *

Lying in hospital, the days dragged on and on. He was still there when Christmas rolled around. It was a time my father once talked a little about, after something had triggered his memory, perhaps the Christmas carols playing in the background. There was one Christmas he would never forget, he said. It was in Brussels during the war.

'I can still hear the German nurses singing carols as they walked through the hospital on Christmas Day.' He seemed to be almost transported back in time as he spoke. 'They came down our particular ward and stopped at each bed. Not just at their own people, they came around to each of us, singing, and giving us gifts.'

It didn't quite fit with my picture of the war, to visualise injured POWs receiving presents from German nurses.

'The townspeople of Brussels were aware that we were in this hospital and they sent in various gifts for us.'

'Like what sorts of things?' I said.

'Oh, bottles of wine, biscuits, chocolates,' he said, no doubt remembering just how much of a treat those things had been at the time.

'When they came through our ward, the carol they were singing was Silent Night. They were singing in German of course,' he said with a faraway look, as he tried to remember how it went.

'Stille Nacht, Heilige Nacht,' he sang, slightly out of tune. 'It went something like that,' he said, sounding not entirely sure, before slipping back into reverie.

At the time, he had thought it was quite a reasonable sort of Christmas. Clearly his expectations had lowered considerably since the previous year when he'd spent Christmas at RAF Catterick. Unfortunately his expectations were going to have to lower even further.

Chapter 12

'Close the shutters'

I have a rendezvous with Death
When Spring brings back blue days and fair.

Alan Seeger

From Brussels hospital my father was sent to a civilian prison in Antwerp during the severe winter of 1942. He had no idea why he had been sent there. Conditions were extremely harsh. He was familiar with his rights according to the Geneva Convention regarding the treatment of prisoners of war, and being placed in what he later called 'the Gestapo-controlled, non-military Antwerp SS prison' was a clear violation of these rights. My father never knew why he was sent to this particular hospital prison and it remained a lifelong mystery to him.

Within the Antwerp hospital prison he was put in a ward with a group of about twenty-five Jewish prisoners. Not knowing the horrors of the concentration camps that were taking place at the time, he had a first-hand indication of how badly the Jewish people were being treated. The Jewish prisoners in his ward had been slave labourers and were, he said, 'reduced to physical wrecks.' It was quite apparent that they had experienced horrific treatment. Injuries from rifle butts were plain to see. They had been brought to Antwerp hospital prison in an attempt to get them back into a state of health where they could be put back into working parties again. My father was appalled by what he saw. 'How could human beings treat other human beings in such a manner?' he said years later, still aghast at the memory. His time in Antwerp showed him that the hardships he endured, paled in comparison to what many others had to survive.

At mealtimes my father would have only eaten a few mouthfuls of his meal, when the sound of his Jewish friends desperately scraping the bottom of their bowls would permeate the ward. It was a sound, he said, that had to be heard, to be believed. My father was so moved by their plight that he wanted to do something, *anything*, to help them. He noticed one of the German guards wasn't like the others, appearing to feel sorry for the Jewish prisoners. One day my father persuaded this guard to let him share some of his rations with the Jewish prisoners and was amazed by the scale of their gratitude. It was as if they had forgotten what it was like to have someone treat them kindly. As he talked to the Jewish prisoners, he learned how terribly they had been treated and found it traumatic to hear their stories. One of the Jewish prisoners had a badly swollen, septic knee. The German doctors operated on him right there in the ward without giving him any anaesthetic. As they cut open his leg, his screams rang out like the howls of a tortured animal. It was obvious that he was suffering the worst possible kind of pain. My father was never able to forget those screams. They haunted him for the rest of his life.

His experiences in Antwerp were amongst the most traumatic of his time at war. He hardly ever spoke of his experiences there, preferring to 'close the shutters' on that period. I suppose it was his coping mechanism for trying to deal with something so disturbing. While he did share a little of what he'd witnessed there, I suspect there was a lot more he could have said. But it must have been either too painful to remember, or too awful to tell an innocent daughter, or both. When he did talk about his time in Antwerp, it was to describe some of the traumatic things the Jewish prisoners had experienced, not the trauma he had endured. I'm curious to know more about his time in Antwerp, but I suspect he had perfected the art of forgetting with this particular chapter of his life.

In 1987, the New Zealand government officially recognised that my father had been 'illegally detained for an extended period under conditions closely comparable with those prevailing in the Nazi concentration camps.' In a statement that he provided to the government about his time in Antwerp, my father wrote, 'in short, a hellish atmosphere prevailed in the Antwerp SS Prison.' He provided a brief description of the inhumane treatment he had witnessed and the scars it left him with, before concluding with a line that is my father through and through: 'I wish to place on record that I harbour no animosity whatsoever towards the German nation.'

* * *

In spring 1942, with his leg still in plaster up to his hip, my father was finally let out of the gruesome Antwerp prison and sent to Germany. Virtually all captured allied airmen were required to pass through 'Durchgangslager der Luftwaffe', known as Dulag Luft, at Oberursel near Frankfurt. Here they were interrogated before being assigned to a permanent prison camp. While the Germans neglected to question many prisoners of war, they made an exception with naval and air force personnel, interrogating nearly all of them. The Luftwaffe knew the allied aircrews could potentially be an invaluable source of strategic information to inform things such as searchlight position.

Arriving in Oberursel after a long journey from Belgium, my father looked out the window at the quaint, little village. As they drove into Dulag Luft, past the large white rocks on the front lawn, he stared wide-eyed at the large prison camp before him. This transit camp had been purpose-built on the site of an old government poultry farm. It was surrounded by 12 ft tall, parallel fences about 10 ft apart, with trenches and barbed wire entangled between them. Watchtowers were spaced around the camp at 100 yd intervals. Inside they headed towards the main building, a stone house. Nearby, wooden barrack blocks were spaced out over the level ground.

Shown to a temporary cell, my father was searched thoroughly by a *Feldwebel* (Sergeant), before being allocated POW number 39620. From there he was taken to a room in the interrogation centre in the stone house. In due course a man dressed in RAF uniform entered the room. He introduced himself as a RAF Squadron Leader and asked my father where he was from.

'I shan't be revealing any information,' my father said.

'Oh, you don't need to worry here,' the man said, oozing friendliness.

Speaking in perfect English, he claimed that my father had been granted the privilege of being allowed to speak with him first. My father looked at him dubiously as his questions casually continued.

'What squadron are you with?'

'As I said, I will not be revealing any information.'

My father knew only to well that, according to the Geneva Convention, he was only required to give his name, rank and serial number. His Air Force training had prepared him for this very situation.

'Listen, there's really no need to worry. There are no bugs here. I've checked everything.'

My father was unconvinced. He sat there, looking straight ahead and said nothing. The man was clearly a put-up. Undeterred, he kept on with question after question. But my father stubbornly refused to engage with him, and just kept reiterating that he was not prepared to reveal anything. The man eventually gave up. The Germans typically didn't go to great lengths to get prisoners to talk. With so many POWs passing through Dulag Luft, it was easier to wait for one who would talk, rather than try to break a prisoner who stubbornly refused.

Next my father was given an International Red Cross form and told that if he completed it, the Red Cross would inform his family back home that he was alive and well. A completed form would also

supposedly ensure prompt delivery of Red Cross parcels. He looked
at the form. It started off harmlessly, asking for name, rank and serial
number. Simple personal questions such as date of birth, and mother
and father's names followed. But then there were questions enquiring
the type of aircraft flown, point of departure, bomb load, name of
squadron, and so forth. My father wasn't taken in by the phoney
questionnaire and left it completely blank.

Finally, realising they could get nothing out of him, he was taken
along Hohemarkstrasse to Reserve Lazarett Hohemark, Dulag Luft's
hospital for wounded prisoners. There he joined many other wounded
Air Force prisoners.

The first thing a fellow prisoner said to him was, 'I hope you didn't
tell that chap at the interrogation centre anything?'

Everyone looked at my father, wondering if he had fallen for the
fraud in the RAF uniform.

'No I didn't,' he said, feeling pleased with himself. 'I had been
warned of his existence.'

Everyone looked relieved and, after introductions, he was soon
getting to know the other prisoners. My father had to remain at this
transit camp hospital until he was allocated a permanent POW camp.
He was surprised by how well they were treated at Dulag Luft, guessing
the Germans were trying to soften them up for further questioning.
The prisoners felt sure the place was bugged in the hope the Germans
could glean any information they might reveal amongst themselves. In
case anyone was listening, they liked to talk provocatively about things
like aircraft that flew at supersonic speeds.

* * *

After spending a few weeks at Dulag Luft, my father was sent to a
large POW hospital, known as Reserve-Lazarett 1249, administered
by Stalag IX C. Located in a former agricultural college at the end

of the village of Obermassfeld-Grimmenthal, it stood beside a stream in a wide valley. The large, reddish, three-storey stone building, with bars on the lower windows, had previously been a hostel for the Hitler Youth. I don't know if my father knew anything of the history of his latest prison, or that it was Hitler's fifty-third birthday the day he arrived there: 20 April 1942. Certainly no one knew then that in exactly three years and ten days Hitler would be dead by his own hand.

Inside the hospital, my father was led into a spacious tiled hallway. Off to the right was a light and airy ward filled with hospital beds for about ninety men. Wounded prisoners lay on their greying, infrequently laundered sheets. There were dozens more beds on the floors above. Along with the wards, the hospital was divided into medical officer quarters, operating rooms, guard quarters, a plaster room for casts, and an x-ray room. German medical orderlies patrolled the hospital night and day. The facility catered mainly for orthopaedic cases. Many of the patients were RAF personnel shot down during raids over Europe; others were from infantry regiments of the British Army and had been imprisoned from as far back as the Norwegian Campaign and the Battle of France. With nothing else to do, my father began to get to know the men in his ward. As they exchanged anecdotes, incredible stories of survival were gradually disclosed. One of the men had been one of only two survivors of a brutal massacre in the French village, Le Paradis, where ninety-nine members of the 2nd Battalion were led across the road to a wall and machine-gunned down in cold blood. Traumatised prisoners had no alternative but to endure the psychological aftermath of their experiences. There was of course no counselling or support provided to POWs within these hospital prisons.

Even though it was now many months since my father had broken his lower leg bones, they still weren't healing properly. After examining him, a German doctor decided that they needed to be reset. It was a lifelong frustration for my father that this German doctor saw fit to re-break his broken bones. And he didn't do nearly as good a job of setting them, as had the kindly Austrian doctor in Leuven. Then, even once the bones had been reset, they still didn't knit together properly. There was, however, about to be a silver lining to having a badly injured leg.

Not long after arriving at the POW hospital at Obermassfeld, a Swiss Red Cross party visited. The powder blue uniforms of the Swiss doctors marked them apart from their German counterparts. The British doctors at Obermassfeld presented a number of cases for the visitors to review. By good fortune my father's leg plaster had recently been temporarily removed. When it was his turn to be examined, his unsightly, raw-looking wound was clearly on display. The assessment team decided that his injury was bad enough to qualify for a place on the list of prisoners who could potentially be repatriated in exchange for German prisoners. Men so severely injured that they could no longer be considered a military threat, qualified for the possibility of future medical repatriation. However it would be some time before a repatriation agreement would be reached between the warring parties. So long, in fact, that by the time the first exchange finally took place in Europe, fifty of the prisoners selected for repatriation had died in captivity.

My father was becoming increasingly concerned about the failure of his leg to heal. All these months and the bones still hadn't knitted. He had a keen interest in nutritional matters and as a champion cyclist knew a little about sports nutrition. It occurred to him that the meagre diet he was receiving as a POW would be nutritionally deficient. He knew that he wasn't getting the calcium or other nutrients required for optimal bone health. By this time, he was receiving regular Red Cross parcels that contained small tins of cheese. He decided to try and exchange some of his items for other prisoners' tins of cheese. After each issue of Red Cross parcels, he usually managed to get about seven tins. He mixed the cheese with the ration of potatoes they received each day. After mashing it together in a dixie, he would leave it on the hot water pipes in the bathroom until evening. Night after night his evening meal consisted of lukewarm cheesy mashed potatoes. Eventually, 'it seemed to do the trick.' His bones started to knit together again, and his leg finally began to heal properly. At long last he was out of plaster for good.

Delighted to be able to exercise again, he gradually managed to get his knee moving normally once more. His ankle slowly improved, although it was never again able to move through its full range of motion, bothering him from time to time for the rest of his life. Everyday he walked around and around the camp trying to get stronger and fitter. With his rudimentary health and fitness knowledge and trademark bloody-minded determination, my father managed to rehabilitate himself admirably. Like other POWs, he was incredibly grateful to the Red Cross for their parcels. Not only did they provide hope, they prevented the prisoners from being reduced to walking skeletons. Alone, the food rations they received in the camp would have kept them all in a perpetual state of hunger. A few pieces of black bread per day were all they were usually given, supplemented with barley or potato soup.

My father was no longer able to keep a daily diary. The Germans told the prisoners that if they were caught with any writings, it would be the last time anyone would hear about them. Many details of his day-to-day life at Obermassfeld are sketchy and limited to the anecdotes he shared later in life. He never mentioned anything about celebrating Christmas Day in his POW Camp in Germany. I don't suppose there was anything particularly memorable to report. One thing seems certain: Christmas on the other side of the world was getting progressively worse.

* * *

In spring 1943, the camp at Obermassfeld became overcrowded and my father was amongst a group of convalescents moved to a medical

POW camp at Kloster Haina, south of Kassel. Reserve Lazarett Stalag IX A/H* was set up inside the grounds of a Cistercian Abbey, which had been used as a mental health facility for the previous 300 years. The Abbey, an early gothic building with a towering steeple, was at the heart of the old-fashioned village of Haina. A picturesque green forest of fir and birch trees surrounded the hamlet. The Wohra River meandered by in the shadow of the mountain, Hohes Lohr. At any other time Haina would have been a beautiful setting to enjoy.

My father surveyed the ancient grey-brown stone buildings that had become his latest prison. Two layers of barbed wire enclosed the camp, with guards patrolling in between. Only some of the buildings were used for the wounded POWs. Others continued their pre-war operation as an asylum for the mentally ill. He walked across the cobblestone yard in front of his three-storey building. Fellow prisoners paced like caged birds. Beyond the barbed wire, a forest slope beckoned, but it would have to wait. First he needed to further strengthen his injured leg.

The prisoners at Stalag IX A/H were mostly 'als D-U' (als Dienstunfähig) meaning they were unable to work. These men had all been seriously wounded. Some had fallen out of crashed planes. Others had weathered numerous battles. For the POWs at Stalag IX A/H, their war was definitely over. All that was left to do was to wait for medical repatriation, or the end of the war, whichever came first. Looking at the other prisoners, my father could see that he didn't have much to complain about. A number were blind, burned or had lost a limb. But they seemed cheerful enough. It was hard to believe their good spirits in such unenviable circumstances. The monastery, Kloster Haina, had been chosen as a POW hospital camp because not only could it house prisoners, it had an existing medical centre that could aid the wounded prisoners. The Germans had opened a Centre

---

* The National Archives, UK: WO 208/3293, WO 224/172, WO 311/598, TS 26/505, WO 311/197

for the Blind at Kloster Haina, to which all eye injuries were sent. A British ophthalmic surgeon, Dr Charters, was in charge of the eye centre. Remarkably, a Braille school was established there with several teachers working with the blind POWs. Another group of POWs were amputees, as the facility also had a focus on orthopaedics and rehabilitation. My father was one of more than 300 patients housed in two buildings with large red crosses painted on their roofs. Hundreds more sick and mentally ill German patients were housed in separate quarters amongst the park like grounds.

Dad talked reasonably freely about his time as a prisoner of war when I was growing up. I got the impression it had been a memorable time in his life, certainly a formative one. I remember one of our conversations well.

'Camp life wasn't as bad as you might expect,' he said.

I nodded enthusiastically. I'd heard some of his POW tales before and from them, combined with my impressions from *Hogan's Heroes*, I imagined it had almost been a bit of fun at times.

'Well, it was no picnic,' he said, realising that perhaps he had painted an overly bright picture. 'But at least, as non-commissioned officers, we didn't have to work.'

'How did you fill in the time?'

'We had a well-stocked library. I remember reading *The Republic* by Plato.'

That certainly sounded like something the wise, mature man I knew would read, but I was surprised to hear that he had delved into such a heavy philosophical tome in his early twenties. Then again, when you're putting your life on the line, fighting in the name of freedom, reading Plato's critical view of democracy may have seemed highly relevant to an enquiring mind.

'And we were able to exercise in the precincts of the camp. We played sport and various games. Life passed reasonably quickly,' dad said, giving the impression it hadn't all been bad.

'We had our Red Cross parcels coming regularly and we received letters from home.'

What I didn't know then was that dad's war stories were the glass half full ones that he cared to remember and share. Along with these, and the dramatic escape narratives that came to define prison life in the post war years, I was left with a false impression of the reality of life behind barbed wire. The truth was, of course, that life in captivity was nothing short of grim. But my father knew it could have been a lot worse, as it was for many others. British and Commonwealth prisoners enjoyed a special status within the prison camps of Germany. Unlike many allied prisoners, their countries were not occupied by the Axis. The Germans knew that the treatment of their own men in captivity depended in part on the way they cared for the British and Commonwealth prisoners. My father found the treatment they received also depended a lot on the individual personalities of their captors.

An elderly German doctor, Dr Zeiss, was the commandant at Kloster Haina. Having managed the mental health facility for many years prior to the war, Stalag IX A/H now also fell under his jurisdiction. The British doctors found Dr Zeiss to be a mild and rather benign doctor, somewhat unsuited to his military role leading a POW hospital. The same couldn't be said about his assistant Dr Jung. In his mid-thirties, Dr Jung appeared to believe far more in Nazi standards and methods for dealing with POWs. Unfortunately for the prisoners, Dr Jung exercised strong control over them since Dr Zeiss was busy running the mental health hospital and was often unavailable.

Dr Jung's most distinctive feature was the vivid duelling scar on his right cheek. What little hair he had was dark and close-cropped. Some of the prisoners thought he looked a bit like Mussolini. It didn't take them long to figure out that Dr Jung, while usually quite polite, could become quite unpleasant in order to get his own way. The British doctors often felt frustrated by the way he would unjustifiably interfere with the comfort of the patients or withhold medical supplies. His aggressive Nazi spirit regularly resulted in hardship for the patients and they wished he was more like the humane Dr Zeiss.

To help pass the time, the prisoners liked to put on their own entertainment. A group of men formed a band using instruments provided by the YMCA. Another group formed a choir. A German man, who worked at the stalag, sometimes played the piano that sat on the stage in the dining hall. The prisoners enjoyed his skilful renditions of songs they all knew. Many of the prisoners had been at Kloster Haina for over a year and had tales to tell about how they'd amused themselves during the long winter months. On Boxing Day, a group of men had put on a performance of 'Snow White and the Seven D-U's.' A Canadian prisoner played the role of Prince Charming, a Derby lad was Snow White, and seven amputees played the D-U's. It was, by all accounts, a scream and one of the best shows to grace the stage at Stalag IX A/H. Another favourite anecdote was about the time they had gone outside in the snow and built a large liner with a Red Cross on it to take them home. The way prisoners made the best of their circumstances, despite the overwhelmingly negative nature of life as a POW, testifies to the resilience of the human spirit.

As unpopular as Dr Jung was, he occasionally displayed a softer side. One day when a group of prisoners were playing 'housie housie', Dr Jung entered the room. The ranking officer called the men to attention. Dr Jung at once ordered the 'carry on' and then stayed and watched the game. He remarked that they knew it as 'Lotto' and said it was better played with a litre of beer. The ranking officer agreed and smilingly suggested beer might be allowed. That evening the prisoners were amazed when they each received a bottle of beer.

Another day, a group of patients persuaded Dr Jung to let them go swimming at a nearby lake, ostensibly on medical grounds. It started out as an unusually pleasant day, but things went horribly wrong when one of the prisoners drowned. When Dr Jung heard that there had been a tragic accident at the lake, he immediately headed there on his motorcycle. But luck wasn't on anyone's side that day. Dr Jung had an accident en route to the lake. I don't suppose the prisoners knew that Dr Jung was also the local General Practitioner in Haina, or that he had a wife and three young children. Nor would they probably have known that he had joined the Nazi party in 1931 and worked in military hospitals in Belgium, France and Russia during the first two years of the war. But having to coexist as enemies, in less than ideal circumstances, my father and many of the prisoners could see that they were all, first and foremost, human beings.

It was remarkable what one could get used to. Strangely my father developed a lifelong love of stale bread having had to eat it every day during his time in captivity. When I was growing up, stale bread was never thrown away at our house. It was always preserved for dad, who largely refused to eat bread any other way for the rest of his life. Along with their perpetual hunger, boredom was another constant companion. Many found the days interminable and, with little to do, life could be mind-numbingly dull. It was certainly a time that provided the opportunity for long reflection and soul-searching. The prisoners were young men with unlimited time to ponder matters mundane and grand. I often wondered if my father became such a lateral thinker because of his long period of incarceration at such a formative age. Even though I'm told he was a fairly serious youngster before going to war, I expect it played a key part in shaping him into the deep-thinking, spiritual man I knew. He chose to view endless time for reflection as not entirely a bad thing. In writing about his time in captivity later in life, dad was philosophical about the experience: 'Methinks there was some needed direction in all this.'

* * *

Within the POW camp, my father was surrounded by men who had suffered unspeakable trauma; men like his Canadian friend Larry. A number of the Canadians wounded on the beaches of Dieppe in August 1942, ended up at Kloster Haina. One of them was Lance Corporal Lawrence Milton Barjarow, a Canadian my father knew as Larry. Having lost an eye during the Dieppe raid, he had been sent to the eye centre at Kloster Haina. My father got on well with Larry and they struck up a tight friendship. Larry had left behind his wife and five small children when he enlisted with the Royal Canadian Engineers and left for war. One of five boys himself, two of Larry's brothers had paid the supreme sacrifice in the First World War. Larry hoped his family weren't worrying too much about him, and tried to reassure them in letters he wrote from the POW Camp at Kloster Haina.

17 November 1942
Dear Mother
Just to let you know I am getting along fine and there is no need to worry. Getting the best of care and able to get out and around. I was out on a walk this morning and I sure had a good appetite when we got back in. We had our first bit of snow yesterday. Just a bit of a flurry. It is very lively scenery around here and puts me in mind of home with its wooded valleys and hills.

Like my father, Larry left out the harsher realities of life as a POW in his letter, which was published in the local newspaper at the time. But when he was liberated in 1945, he spoke more candidly to a reporter: 'Every time I see a canary in a cage now, I feel like letting it out,' he said, providing a glimpse into how it had felt to be imprisoned.

Friendship was a powerful ally in the close confines of a POW camp. Another good mate my father had at the time was Scottish soldier Bill Watson. Larry, Bill and my father relied on each other for friendship and moral support. It made a big difference to befriend like-minded people. The relentless proximity to dozens of men you may otherwise not have chosen to be around, required high levels of tolerance at times. The upside to having so many people on hand, though, was that it was always easy to make up football and cricket teams. The YMCA had delivered sporting gear to the prisoners. Boxing gloves, softballs, footballs and table-tennis balls were made available. Sometimes the games got serious and 'international events' were staged between the British and the Commonwealth.

In time my father got fitter and his leg got stronger. With unlimited time to ruminate, he thought a lot about escaping. He and Bill, who 'had similar ideas', would plot and scheme together when no one was around. They had to be careful not to be overheard because some of the prisoners, fearing reprisals to all of the prisoners in the camp, would immediately report any escape plans to the German guards. Knowing dad, I'm not at all surprised he wasn't content to sit around and wait for the end of the war. Despite knowing he would be risking his life if he attempted escape, his 'leave no stone unturned' approach to life came to the fore. Besides, his training in the Air Force had included instruction in the art of escape and evasion, and captured servicemen were expected to attempt escape wherever possible.

Furthermore, life at Kloster Haina had greatly deteriorated. Dr Zeiss had been claimed by his department and discharged from the military at the beginning of summer in 1943. The prisoners felt sure that Dr Zeiss would have been more than happy to leave his post. He had often seemed overwhelmed by the Nazi machine. Dr Jung had now risen to the position of commandant and a continuous state of uncertainty and insecurity plagued the lazarett (hospital). With Dr Jung unilaterally in charge, my father was more desperate than ever to try and get out of the place. He and Bill began to closely observe the way the prison was guarded, hoping to find a loophole they could exploit. They imagined themselves on the other side of the barbed wire, heading towards freedom, and thought about what they would need to take with them, secretly stashing away dry rations for such an eventuality.

If my father could make it out of Stalag IX A/H he hoped never to return, so he began to get the names and addresses of some of the other prisoners. He still had his little brown book with his handwritten English–German Dictionary at the front. When the guards weren't looking, he would get his cobbers to write their names and addresses in it. The dozens of men who wrote their contact details in his little brown book came from England, Scotland, Wales, Northern Ireland, Canada, Australia and New Zealand.

Throughout my father's time at war, the threat of death was ever present. He had already had several close encounters with death. Now he knew that if he was to attempt escape, the chance of being recaptured and killed was high. Judging by the two poems that he had scrawled in his little brown book, alongside the contact details of his fellow prisoners, death and existential matters were top of mind. First there is the poem *Crossing the Bar* by Alfred, Lord Tennyson.

> *Sunset and evening star,*
> *And one clear call for me!*
> *And may there be no moaning of the bar,*
> *When I put out to sea,*
>
> *But such a tide as moving seems asleep,*
> *Too full for sound and foam,*
> *When that which drew from out the boundless deep*
> *Turns again home.*
>
> *Twilight and evening bell,*
> *And after that the dark!*
> *And may there be no sadness of farewell,*
> *When I embark;*

> *For tho' from out our bourne of Time and Place*
> *The flood may bear me far,*
> *I hope to see my Pilot face to face*
> *When I have crost the bar.*

And following this, he had scrawled a poem by Countee Cullen:

> *I have a rendezvous with Life,*
> *In days I hope will come,*
> *Ere youth has sped, and strength of mind,*
> *Ere voices sweet grow dumb.*
> *I have a rendezvous with Life,*
> *When Spring's first heralds hum.*
> *Sure some would cry it's better far*
> *To crown their days with sleep*
> *Than face the road, the wind and rain,*
> *To heed the calling deep.*
> *Though wet nor blow nor space I fear,*
> *Yet fear I deeply, too,*
> *Lest Death should meet and claim me ere*
> *I keep Life's rendezvous.*

Lastly there is a quote written in someone else's handwriting.

> *There is something in us that can be without us, and will be after us,*
> *though indeed it hath no history of what it was before us, and cannot*
> *tell how it entered into us.*
>
> *Sir Thomas Browne*

I picture my father reading these words over and over as he began to plot and plan his escape from Stalag IX A/H, and imagine what freedom on the other side of the wire might feel like.

Chapter 13

'The true story of Kriegsgefangener number 39620'

Yea, though I walk through the valley of the shadow of death, I will fear no evil: for thou art with me; thy rod and thy staff they comfort me.

Psalm 23:4

If there was one thing I was enormously proud of when I was a kid, it was that my father had tried to escape from a POW Camp in Nazi Germany. I think he was pretty chuffed about it too because he was happy to tell us all about it. I thought it was the most marvellous and exciting story I had ever heard. And dad was a wonderful storyteller. I remember one day at bedtime asking my father to tell me a story. As usual he obliged, but this time he departed from his usual repertoire of *Grimm's Fairy Tales*. Kneeling at my bedside, he cleared his throat as he prepared to start the story.

'This is the true story of Kriegsgefangener number 39620,' he said, sounding serious.

'Who?' I asked

'Me,' he said, smiling.

I smiled too, realising I was about to hear something rather special.

With his trademark formality, he told me that after he had languished in POW camps for two years waiting for his broken leg to heal, he gradually became strong enough to contemplate escaping. He had my full attention. I'd seen the movie *Escape from Colditz* and in my mind, my father's story seemed like a movie where he was the star.

He and his Scottish friend Bill decided to make a few plans together to get out of the place.

'But,' he said, lowering his voice, 'we had to be particularly careful to keep our plans to ourselves. Secrecy was essential.'

He explained that in the camp, if anything like an escape took place, the Germans came down very heavily on everyone. All the privileges would be stopped. Previous escape attempts at Haina had resulted in Dr Jung locking everyone inside for days, stopping the hot water supply and preventing them from accessing their Red Cross parcels.

'There were prisoners amongst us who would have readily given us away. So we kept our escape plans pretty much to ourselves,' he said, before pausing for a moment to recall.

'Actually, there were one or two people who we knew we could trust implicitly, who helped us.'

I was hanging on his every word. He described how, unobtrusively, they made their plans towards the great day when they would be on *the other side*.

'We acquired a map, a compass, and two army water bottles from a trusted source. We surreptitiously stored away rations – broken biscuits, rolled oats, chocolate raisins – from our great lifesaver, the Red Cross parcels.'

The way he always said that, I was left with the impression that his life had literally depended on these parcels of gold. The camp he was in had an inner camp that was surrounded by a high barbed wire entanglement. Beyond that there was a no man's land where the guards patrolled that was enclosed by a further high barbed wire entanglement. To escape they would have to get across both barbed wire fences. They decided daytime was their best chance of getting out. Having observed the movements of the guard in their part of the camp, they noted that every second day he was required to open the main gate at 3.30pm for a party of prisoners taking out rubbish. While the guard did this, he was unsighted on a segment of the perimeter for almost two minutes.

My eyes got wider as dad's tone became deadly serious. 'Would we have time to breach the inner wire, cross the no man's land and scale the outer fence? We thought so.' Then he added with a twinkle in his eye, 'The alternative of a bullet in our rear quarters, we ignored.'

I marvelled at his audacity.

The day of their escape finally arrived. Freedom beckoned.

'At 3.00pm a quick check showed a yawning, unsuspecting guard. At 3.25pm we were casually in position awaiting a relayed signal. Our trusted aide was wishing he was coming with us.'

I pictured them waiting tensely. The minutes must have felt like an eternity.

'Then it was "go",' dad said suddenly.

The next few moments passed in a blur of action. They breached the first entanglement with some assistance from their helper, who then passed their bag through to them. Then they dashed through no man's land with pounding hearts to the high entanglement on the outside. The only way over it was to climb one of the posts with bare hands. Dimly conscious of bleeding hands from the barbed wire, they were quickly up and over the top, before dropping to the ground. Rapidly they melted into the nearby bush, where, out of sight, they could finally stop to catch their breath.

'Everything was quiet. We had made it.'

I lay listening, enthralled, barely able to believe it was all actually true.

'One of our trusted people was part of the garbage disposal team that day and he managed to delay them a bit.'

Dad's friend had deliberately turned up at the gate for rubbish duty without his cap on. The Germans were sticklers for people being properly attired when going out of the camp and the guard sent him back to get his cap.

'We had to immediately put as much distance between us and the camp as possible, not knowing whether our escape had been discovered.'

I loved the far away look on my father's face when he was telling a story. He was often in his own world, but when he told a story he was simultaneously fully present yet completely unconscious of everything around him.

Realising it was getting late, dad said, 'But the subsequent events and our days of freedom are another story.'

He gave me a kiss good night and promised to tell me the rest of the story the next evening.

I wonder if he remembered that in his escape bag, along with his supplies, he had taken his little brown notebook with all the names of his POW camp mates. The only time my father dared to make a diary entry during his two years in captivity was once, in this notebook, during his time on the run. This is what he hastily scrawled somewhere deep in the bush in the heart of Germany.

July 1943 – Bill Watson and self journey forth into the wilderness on July 24th. Initial stages forced but quite successful. My leg is fairly sore with all the unaccustomed exercise, but should improve. Greatly troubled by hordes of ants. Horse flies show their teeth. Our POW broth tasted fine. Fairly difficult finding water as most of the wells have dried up. The good earth is not such a good bed, not enough give and take for our liking. Walked through a wonderful glen this morning. It was grand scenery; also saw some small roebuck deer. Shy wild creatures, they make plenty of noise when they career through the bush. Early morning rather chilly in spite of a ground sheet each and plenty of 'woollies'. However the midday sun has been almost tropical these last few days and we have been heartfully thankful whenever the big dark thunderclouds, so common in this country, cover the sun.

That's all he ever wrote while on the run in Germany. He mustn't have had another opportunity to put pen to paper. He did however have time the following evening, to resume his story.

'So you'd made it out of the camp, what happened next?' I asked, settling down as I keenly anticipated the rest of his escape story.

'Yes. We were free. But we knew that as soon as our absence was detected we would be tracked by dogs, so the first thing we had to do was find some water to cross, to put the dogs off our scent.'

They kept walking until evening, not seeing a soul. Then they hid in an area of undergrowth and rested for an hour or two until it got dark.

'When do you think the German guards figured out that you were missing?'

'Well, we hoped with any luck we would have until the next morning before the hue and cry began. We'd arranged stand-ins for the evening count,' he said, explaining their beds had been dummied to make it look as though they were in them.

'At nightfall we set off again, trying to get as far away as possible from the camp.'

'How did you know which way to go?'

'We had compasses and maps that we'd obtained in the camp.'

They carried on walking all that night and became extremely thirsty. It was the middle of summer and the weather was fine and warm. Their plan was to travel by night and find a place to hide during the day that was handy to water. That way they could take full water bottles into their hiding spot and know where to refill them again before the nighttime trek.

'We managed to find water on most occasions but it wasn't easy.'

'How did it feel to have escaped?'

Dad let out a deep breath and smiled broadly. 'We really enjoyed the feeling of freedom. And we had some interesting times in the midst of Germany's great outdoors.'

It sounded like it had all been a grand adventure to begin with.

'We hid up one day in a huge corn field.'

The outskirts were starting to be harvested so Bill and my father hid on the other side of the field, well away from the workers. It didn't occur to them until later that they could have been eating the corn and saving their own rations. They spent the day in their makeshift camp in the cornfields and could hear the Germans talking to one another, and machinery whirring. Then in the evening, they began their walk again, heading towards Belgium.

'If we got close to a village, the dogs would start barking. We kept our fingers crossed that the dogs wouldn't wake the villagers.'

They typically walked for seven or eight hours each night. One day they couldn't find anywhere suitable to hide, eventually finding a place where bricks were dried in three feet high kilns.

'We hid inside the kilns, lying on the bricks, which were terribly hard.'

I squirmed in my comfortable bed, trying to imagine what lying on bricks felt like.

That morning, while they tried to get some sleep, Bill and my father overheard a couple of nearby workers talking and realised they were speaking French. They debated whether to make contact with them, thinking they may well be French prisoners who had been brought from France to work.

'Eventually we decided that we would risk it and, sure enough, they were French.'

I marvelled at the risk they had taken.

'We had to trust them of course that they wouldn't enlighten the Germans. But they seemed very friendly and they brought us food, and a bed. And they were really quite amazed and excited that we were there.'

The day went on and nothing transpired, no Germans came. As they were about to set off that evening, Bill and my father thanked their new French friends.

'They gave us directions and food and wished us well on our journey.'

I was trying to visualise the whole scenario. I still thought it sounded like something out of a movie.

'So that was a rather strange event that took place as well,' dad said, sounding as though he was still surprised by it himself.

'We contemplated trying to board a train, and we actually went to one particular spot where we thought we might be able to get on a train, but it didn't look very safe, so we didn't get on,' he said, sounding fairly certain that it wouldn't have been a good idea.

'Another night we found some beetroot fields, sugar beet. The Germans grew a lot of sugar beet and we thought we'd try those for eating, which turned out to be a bit of a mistake. I didn't eat much of it but my Scots companion had quite a good feed of it and it upset him very much and he was extremely ill with it,' dad said, losing the adventurous tone and sounding deeply concerned all of sudden.

'All in all, we had spent seven or eight days of freedom trying to get somewhere. But then I became very concerned about my companion who was so ill and I thought I'd better try and get help for him.

'And my injured leg wasn't standing up very well to the continued walking. So we thought the best thing to do was make contact with the Germans.'

My heart sank. Their situation must have been desperate if their best option was to turn themselves in.

'So then we reported to a police station in a local village,' dad said matter-of-factly. Clearly there hadn't been any alternative, with his mate suffering so much.

'What did the Germans do?'

'We were treated rather badly,' he said, not providing any details. 'Eventually we were returned to our former camp. Again we were treated badly. We were threatened, cajoled and told we would be shot. The Germans eventually gave up; gave us two weeks bread and water in solitary confinement and then returned us to the camp where they kept a close eye on us.'

I didn't realise at the time, but dad had completely glossed over the ensuing hardship he had suffered upon recapture. I might never have known anything of the harsh reality of what he had experienced, except that I found some notes he had written among his war related things, which described in more detail what had transpired.

I escaped from the stalag but was recaptured in the town of Korbach, Central Germany. After some extremely torrid treatment and interrogation, we were told that we had committed sabotage and were going to be shot. Then we were thrown into an underground cell, filthy beyond description, an open bucket for urinal purposes, uncleaned from previous occupants, given no water, no food, no blankets. How long we were there I do not now remember. Finally we were told that RAF officers who had also escaped from some other camp had been recaptured and shot by direct order of Hitler himself. What was to be our fate? We knew not. What we did know was that our treatment was in violation of the Geneva Convention of which Germany was a signatory. Some time later, we were sentenced to two weeks bread and water and were incarcerated in a dreadful asylum for that time. Recall is painful even after all this time.

Even though his description was fairly succinct, it had clearly been a hideous time. He had no desire to dwell on this claustrophobic experience, locked in a filthy, underground cell. The Nazis were clearly intent on sending a strong message to would-be escapees. My father was, once again, lucky to escape with his life.

* * *

Having been curious for almost as long as I can remember about my father's POW stories, I visited the site of his former stalag in 2014. Before arriving in Haina, I had exchanged emails with a German gentleman, Mr Wilhelm Helbig, who heads up the association, 'Friends of Kloster Haina'. Arriving at the entrance of the impressive gothic monastery, I was greeted warmly by Mr Helbig. Apparently I looked a lot younger than he was expecting for someone whose father was older than him, and he immediately queried whether it was my father or grandfather who had been in the stalag. It made more sense to him when I explained that my father was nearly 50 when I was born.

Chatting with Mr Helbig as we walked around the former POW Camp, I learned that he was the last living person in Haina who knew anything about the history of Stalag IX A/H. He had been about 10 years old at the time the monastery was used for injured prisoners of war. Very little, he said, ever happened in Haina. Almost all the village men were away at war and life was rather quiet. Having a stalag in the village, housing men from numerous countries, was exciting for young Wilhelm. His father was responsible for the technical equipment in the hospital and Wilhelm was able to accompany him into the stalag. He first started to learn English by speaking to the prisoners of war. Perhaps he even picked up a few words from my father.

His mother was the local postmistress; in fact their home was the village Post Office and he often helped her with her duties after school. Mr Helbig remembered large numbers of Red Cross parcels arriving at his house. Accompanied by a guard, groups of ten prisoners with large trolleys would arrive to collect them. Young Wilhelm proudly used his newfound knowledge of English whenever they came. 'How are you?' he would say while counting out the parcels, 'one, two, three, four...'. The prisoners always tried to have a conversation with him, even though his English was limited. He realised that, despite the Nazi propaganda he had grown up hearing, these strangers were normal young people, just like his parents and brothers. It wasn't just the prisoners who were perpetually hungry, Mr Helbig said. As a boy in Haina, he was hungry for much of the war. He had never forgotten how marvellous the white bread and chocolate tasted when the Americans arrived in 1945.

His brother Heinz was badly injured during the war. His left leg had to be amputated and he needed crutches for the rest of his life. His oldest brother, Wilfried, was drafted into the Luftwaffe and became a pilot. Despite it being forbidden to tell his family where he was stationed, he always found a secret way to let them know. Once he sent a letter from France with dots above certain letters so they could figure out where he was. Towards the end of the war, Wilfried was sent as a paratrooper to the last front on the Rhine and was killed in action on 24 March 1945, two days after his twentieth birthday. He was buried in a nearby garden. After the war, Mr Helbig's parents received a letter from the people whose garden Wilfried was buried in. With great difficulty, they managed to travel from their home in the American occupation zone to his gravesite in the British occupation zone. During the long journey, the final 10km on foot, they decided they would bring their son home, no matter how challenging it was. They ordered a coffin from a local carpenter and found a freight forwarder who was willing to transport them. Once there, they learned that the fallen soldiers had been reburied in a central cemetery. Mr Helbig's father dug into the mass grave with his bare hands. He found his son's body, wrapped in a blanket together with his documents. They took him home and buried him in the cemetery at Kloster Haina, as a fleet of American aircraft flew overhead.

His parents never got over the death of their son. The care of his grave became one of the most important tasks of their life. Despite their grief, Mr Helbig said his parents never held a grudge against the enemy, but never forgave the people who started the war. Mr Helbig's memories of the war reminded me that many Germans were victims of Nazism too. Mr Helbig and I exchanged all the information we had, each learning a little more about this time. He looked visibly relieved when I told him that my father always spoke positively about Germany and German people. He was interested to hear that my father liked to include German expressions in his vernacular from time to time. I was sad when our day together came to an end. A gentle and kindly man, Mr Helbig reminded me somewhat of my father.

Having seen the place that had loomed large in my imagination since childhood, including the barbed wire fences my father had climbed and the forest he had melted into, I headed towards Korbach. I wondered which route Bill and my father had taken as they'd headed hopefully through the undergrowth towards freedom. The largely deserted forest of birch trees, which stretched for miles, was tailor made for moving through undetected. I pictured my father, with his love of the great outdoors, enjoying the trek enormously at first. The boy from Koru probably felt quite at home.

Curious to see the old police station where Bill and dad had turned themselves in eight days later, I navigated through the old centre of Korbach towards Hagenstrasse. In my imagination the police station had always been a small, unimposing building, one of only a handful of unremarkable buildings in a one-horse town. Instead, looming before me was a grand, traditional German building with iconic brown timber frames crisscrossing white walls. Standing stately at the intersection of two wide roads, its grandeur was in keeping with the beautiful, medieval walled city of Korbach, a town largely untouched by world wars.

Gazing at the two-storey former police station, I tried to imagine a swastika hanging down its front. A black and white picture formed in my mind. I strolled around the outside of the mansion viewing it from various vantage points. It was hard to imagine my father having been locked up inside in a filthy, underground cell. Then, as I stood facing the entrance, I paused to imagine my father standing before the home of the local polizei in 1943. The tremendous courage he must surely have needed to climb the stairs and enter the building, not knowing if he would ever exit it alive, suddenly struck me. Perhaps it was the impressive building that helped me to feel the enormity of his predicament. His situation must have been so very dire if, having gone to the trouble of escaping, the only apparent option was to walk inside and turn himself over. My emotions got the better of me as I put myself in my father's shoes and tried to feel the desperation and courage he must have felt. I wondered how Bill Watson fared once he was back in the hands of the Nazis. Had my father persuaded them to give him the medical care he so urgently required, or were they both simply lucky to escape with their lives?

* * *

Having endured their harsh punishment for escaping, Bill and my father were put back in the main camp at Kloster Haina towards the end of summer. It was hard not to feel despondent. Dr Jung was still making their lives miserable. He had been rattled by the escapes and his strong anti-British feelings were more apparent than ever. The days stretched on interminably with no known end in sight. Of course, no-one had any way of knowing when, or if, the war would end. Despite every endeavour to keep accurate news from the prisoners, they had become aware that the Reich was being rocked by the RAF. Typically, prisoners had access to two types of news: the camp broadcast of alleged war developments that the Germans fed them, and the remarkably effective underground news that was spread camp-to-camp via the grapevine.

With the growing power of the British bomber force, the attacks on Germany were increasing in intensity. From his POW Camp, my father sometimes heard bombing raids pounding nearby towns. His experience of these deafening raids was later described in a newspaper article: 'Walker had a close-up experience of the thousand-bomber raid on Kassel in October of last year, and while he was not able to see a great deal of the damage, he said that the "racket and disorder were terrific, and almost beyond imagination."' Mr Helbig also remembered the bombings well. He said during the nighttime raids on Kassel, it had been as light as day in Haina. Countless aircraft flew noisily overhead, dropping bombs, some planes even crashing nearby. As Kassel burned, and two of Mr Helbig's aunts perished in the firestorms, the catastrophic fires lit up the skies for miles.

For my father in his prison, news of the progress the Allies were making provided a glimmer of hope. Now he knew from bitter experience that escape was not his ticket out of there. There was little else to brighten the endless days, the only exception being letters from friends and family. One special letter dad treasured, and preserved among his wartime keepsakes, was a letter from his 'war mum', Josephine Nicholls in Exeter. It had been written on a special purpose aerogramme with English, German and French printed in the top left corner:

Prisoner of War Post

Kriegsgefangenenpost

Service des Prisonniers de Guerre

There are spaces for the sender to fill in rank & name, prisoner of war number, camp name and number, and country. Mrs Nicholls had addressed it to Stalag IX C in Obermassfeld, not knowing he had been moved by this time to Kloster Haina. However his new address had been handwritten over the top in red and purple pencil on arrival in Germany. The envelope had been stamped by the postal censor who had also blacked out several lines in the letter.

Mrs Nicholls, who was about to celebrate her seventy-eighth birthday, had written him a touching letter:

I keep on writing to you and I do hope you will receive my letters. I am trying very hard to live till you come back but it is almost impossible ... Dear laddie, you and Mac were my dearest. God bless and keep you. Knowing you has been a very bright spot in my life, one that would have been very lonely otherwise. It comforts me to go back over days when you were with me. I picture you on a sunny day sitting in a chair in the garden, near the apple tree, reading. I have asked a friend to send you a few books although it seems silly as you will be here soon I hope. I have been asked by his mother to write all I can remember of Mac. What an example he was, always loving and kind. Goodbye from your war Mum. C J Nicholls.

Clearly Mrs Nicholls had benefitted just as much from my father's visits as he had from the home-away-from-home sanctuary she had lovingly provided. Dad was certainly ever so grateful for her kindness and hospitality when he was so far from home during these turbulent years, and I know he never forgot her. When Mrs Nicholls referred to 'Mac', I presume she would have been referring to Robert Ian McChesney, one of dad's friends from the *Akaroa*, who had been killed in an aircraft accident the previous December. Almost all my father's airmen friends were killed in action during the war: Robby, Les Russell, Pat Dyer and now Mac. Nineteen of the thirty-six gunners and observers who sailed on the *Akaroa* with my father died during the war. Recalling the solemn expression on dad's face as he marched in the Dawn Parade, I can now discern the grief he carried for a lifetime, as he remembered his friends who had paid the ultimate price.

I found another of Mrs Nicholls' letters tucked amongst the papers in my father's box of treasures, dated 3 August 1941. Mrs Nicholls had written to my father the same day he set off for his fifteenth op, the last bombing raid he returned safely from. She had sat at her writing desk with a heavy heart, having recently learned that Robby had been killed in a flying accident. My father was unaware of Robby's death and remained so for quite some time. Her letter would have still been in the hands of the Royal Mail when my father crashed in Belgium a couple of days later. It must have been much later that he received Mrs Nicholls' letter, perhaps at his latest address in Germany.

Dear Ian

I am sure you must have heard that dear Robbie was killed on the evening of Tuesday July 22nd in an accident very much the same as the first one he had. The pilot was flying too low and they struck the ground. An inquiry is being held. Anyhow it won't bring Robbie back. He was buried in the churchyard of the village of Byley in Cheshire on Friday after a military service.

I was expecting him down and have his half finished socks ready. It has upset me very much. He was so dear and unselfish. The very last letter I had from him was to remind me not to forget to send the telegram to Scottie for the 16th. Strange – two accidents. The F.O. sent me a very kind letter about it. He had found my letter card on him. I am sending a wreath from all of us – you will like that won't you. It will go as soon as the shops open and should be put on the grave by Friday. I am writing to his mother. Robbie was so upset about his next-door neighbour being killed over in Germany. I tried hard to find out when and where but could not. Well Ian dear, we must try and keep his memory alive in hearts and lives and do what we can to make it easier for others. I am all alone. No one has been here, since you left, to stay.

Tomorrow is a day of remembrance to us. On a bank holiday 4 August 1914 – war was declared. Not one except my daughter and myself are alive who sat and listened to that declaration. Even we had no idea what was ahead for us then. There seems great anxiety about the immediate future. Something is hanging over us. Goodbye my dear boy. God bless and keep you.

> *Most affectionately*
> *Josephine Nicholls.*

Mrs Nicholls' letter to my father evokes the sadness and anxiety everyone lived with at the time. Having been deeply touched by Mrs Nicholls' letter and my father's words about Robby – 'one of the finest chaps who ever lived' – I felt strangely compelled to visit Robby's grave.

It was a fine, spring day the morning I walked among the graves surrounding St John the Evangelist's Church in Byley, Cheshire. Robby's gravesite was behind the church amongst two rows of white RAF headstones. Only 20 years of age, he had been buried alongside other young airmen who had died in the early 1940s. I bent down and placed a rose plant in front of his tombstone, before standing for a while in reflection. The sun beat down on my head, dulling the chill in the air. It was ever so peaceful standing there in the Cheshire countryside, no one to be seen for miles. Apart from the birds chirping as they flitted about, all was silent and still. My father would have been delighted with the beauty and tranquillity of Robby's final resting place. Before leaving, I quietly said my thanks to one of the finest chaps who ever lived. I felt pleased to have carried out Mrs Nicholls' wishes of keeping Robby's memory alive.

In the rich earth of a quiet field in Cheshire, there is a place that is forever New Zealand.

* * *

As well as receiving letters from his war mum, my father also received letters from his family and friends back home. He devoured news of what they were up to and was especially keen to hear news of his older brothers, Ray and Keith, who, after being conscripted into the army, had been sent to the Middle East. Younger brother Cyril had tried to avoid conscription at all costs, saying that he just knew he couldn't kill anyone. He was the 'conscientious objector' in the family. But eventually the law caught up with him and he was made to join the army. I was always fascinated to learn that I had an uncle who had been a conscientious objector. While even the most ardent of anti-war commentators usually concede that, in the end, there was no alternative but to go to war against Hitler; I respect my Uncle's freedom to choose, and can't support anyone being forced to join the army against their wishes.

My father was the only member of the family to volunteer for war service. His brother-in-law Roy had been too young to volunteer when war broke out. Nearer the end of the war, approaching the minimum age, Roy told his father that he would like to enlist. By that time, everyone knew someone who wasn't coming back from the war. Roy's father said to him, 'There's no need for that Roy. I can take you out the back and shoot you *now* if you like.' There was no sugar coating it as a great adventure anymore.

In the letters my father received from home, he learned how the war was impacting life in New Zealand. New Zealanders may have been spared the destruction common in many parts of the world at the time, but life was still disrupted significantly. Many changes had occurred. A nighttime blackout was in force. Tea, coffee, sugar and meat, amongst other things, were rationed to help keep the people of Britain fed. There was widespread speculation and fear about a Japanese invasion. School children, including my mum, had to practice getting into trenches during mock air raids. My father was interested to learn that New Zealand had become an important military base in the Pacific and thousands of American servicemen were stationed there.

If a letter from home could cheer my father up, I can only imagine how he must have felt when the possibility of repatriation presented after more than two long years of captivity. Not long after his recapture and return to the stalag at Kloster Haina, there was talk of imminent repatriation. He didn't allow himself to get his hopes too high. There had been rumours of impending repatriation numerous times. But this time, a repatriation agreement had actually been brokered and, at long last, the first repatriation was set to take place in October 1943. My father was elated when he discovered that he was on the list to be exchanged, man for man, with German prisoners. He was astonished that he was still eligible on medical grounds, given it wasn't long since he had been surreptitiously making his way through the German countryside. However he thought the Germans were probably glad to get rid of him. And he was certainly glad to be about to be rid of his captors.

Chapter 14

'Forgotten what a banana tasted like'

There is music in the midst of desolation.

Laurence Binyon

Sitting on the train on 18 October 1943, no longer under the constant watchful eye of a guard, my father opened a new pale blue notebook and pulled out his lead pencil. On the first line he wrote: *The Best Journey in the World – Repatriation,* and then underlined it. I can sense the elation in the words. They seem to almost jump from the page. He must have felt ecstatic to leave the POW Camp behind.

18 October 1943 – After arriving at 5 o'clock at Obermassfeld, we were searched and departed from the Lazarett at 7 o'clock arriving at the station to find the train was running late. However everyone is in the best of spirits. Our train came in at 11.00pm… consisting of 23 carriages, absolutely first class, every carriage a sleeper. Three tier beds, beautiful clean white sheets, adjustable pillows, sprung mattresses, washing facilities. I was fortunate enough to get a bottom bed and have a good view of the countryside. We quickly boarded the train and at five to twelve our journey has commenced. The boys are all highly elated, particularly as the entire train is sleepers. We had expected to be seated the whole way. We are like millionaires travelling in style. The carriages are fitted with every little luxury, eating tables affixed to the beds, ashtrays set in the wall, small shelves for books, cigarettes etc, big open windows and radio. As I sit here watching the scenery rolling by, my thoughts take me back to the days when I first became a POW – over two years ago now. To be leaving it all behind and going home is almost unbelievable. Perhaps we shall wake up and find it all a dream.

After enduring over two years of primitive conditions in captivity, he was clearly revelling in the luxury of first class train travel courtesy of the Deutsche Reichsbahn. Even little things like 'shelves for books,' seemed wonderful. Understandably he felt like pinching himself to make sure it wasn't all a dream. The men knew it was too early to assume that everything would proceed as planned. Two years earlier, in September 1941, a repatriation agreement between Germany and Britain had fallen through at the last minute due to the disparity in numbers between sides. The prisoners had been duly returned to their POW camps, heartbroken. Since this debacle, Germany had only been prepared to negotiate on the basis of numerical equality. By spring 1943, a final agreement had finally been reached and was now being put into effect. However the repatriates knew that there were several more stages of the process to go before they were officially free.

19 October 1943 – Today we are in Germany – tomorrow sunny France – next week on the Mediterranean and then – who knows? Our freedom is in sight. Strangely enough none of us seem particularly excited. It must be that we cannot yet realise it after the rut we have been in for the past two weary years. Throughout the day we have travelled but apparently have not covered much distance. We passed through Meiningen, Wasungen, Bad Salzungen, but seem to have spent a lot of time stopping outside stations and then going backwards. The German food issue is quite good on this train. The radio has been playing the music of Johann Strauss and Beethoven all day long.

Darkness fell at 6.00pm and after supper at 8.00pm most went to sleep in a most happy frame of mind.

20 October 1943 – Slept very well. This morning we are down near Stuttgart. The scenery in this part, with all the various shades of autumn blended together, makes a truly wonderful sight. Amazingly agricultural this country. Every possible piece of land is cultivated right up to the fringe of the bush, up the hillside and alongside the railways. Passed through Karlsruhe, a very famous old German town. Certainly looked picturesque with its canals, old churches and ancient stone buildings. The people were waving to us, evidently taking us for troops.

Large vineyards lay on either side of the line. Large fields of grapes stretched out for miles, while their rich black clusters of grapes looked very tempting. Here again people waved and appeared very friendly. The weather is fair and sunny and increasingly so the further south we travel.

At about 5.00pm we drew into Mulhausen, which is right in the corner of three borders, German, Swiss and French. At dusk we crossed the line into France. Light was fading and twas too hard to make anything out. Later stopped at Belfort, our first station in France. I heard someone here remark that, 'there must be something in this repat rumour after all.' The French Red Cross, with permission of the German authorities, handed gifts to each man – cake and sandwiches. French bread is very fair. Well on our way now. In a couple of days we should be in Marseilles.

21 October 1943 – Another sound, restful night. Woke up in France and going south. Here, unlike Germany it is far more pastoral. Small villages, stone houses. Passed through Bourg and row upon row of vineyards all in their autumn glory set up on the hillsides. Undoubtedly some of France's famous wine is manufactured here. Throughout the morning the scenery was exhilarating and the weather fine, but later it became dull. Passed through Amberieu-en-Bugey, Mirebel and on into Lyon, one of France's famous cities. Lyon duly impressed us. Full of life and busy people thronging the streets. The city is well spread out. Some very fine old buildings. The river Rhone runs through the centre. Plenty of width and fairly swift (reminded me of the Waikato River). Saw lots of gaily-coloured cottages on the outskirts and after leaving Lyon our course lay along the eastern banks of the Rhone, following the Rhone valley south... Rugged barren hills on either side. Still plenty of vineyards about. Passed through St Rambert D'Albon and Valence where we saw the last of the Rhone. At 6.00pm halted in Avignon. Expect to arrive in Marseilles tomorrow.

October 22 1943 – Stayed up late last night watching night fighters patrolling the railway line. They were flying quite low and were easily visible. Awoke this morning to find ourselves drawn up in Marseilles dockyards... Couldn't see much of the city. Moved further on, right down to the quayside. Plenty of French 'wharfies' about. As the boat had not arrived, the Germans moved us up to various hospitals. Some of the ambulances were of British make.

Passed up through the centre of the shopping district. People thronged the streets. Actually saw a young woman walking along wearing a peg leg. The shops for the most part were like Old Mother Hubbard's cupboard. The French girls seem to use cosmetics rather too freely, or perhaps we have forgotten what civilisation is. Still to come back to the point, we anchored in what was probably a pre-war hotel. It's quite comfortable and after our long journey the beds look rather inviting.

Once again the German issue of food is fairly good although meal hours are very irregular. The sunny Mediterranean is living up to its name and the warmth is a pleasant change. Everyone retired early.

After the monotony of prison life, getting to see some of the country he had spent so long in – even if it was whizzing past at the rate of knots – had been thrilling. Now in Marseille, with no idea where they were being taken to next, this would be his only glimpse of France until I took him there when he was 80.

23 October 1943 – Slept soundly and well. Breakfast at 9am. The grounds are spacious lawns, magnificent old trees, fishponds etc. Despite the fact that we slept so well, everyone feels muggy and tired. It must be the sudden change of climate and probably the sea breeze has something to do with it too. Several German Officers here inspected us.

Have been told that the English exchange is 'proceeding according to plan.' Also that our own contingent embarks early Monday bound for Barcelona. (Bull fights) Several shiploads of German 'Grande Blesse' disembarked here in Marseilles today. Presumably they are the exchange for the English in Sweden. Nothing else of any importance transpired.

My father and his companions learned in Marseille that they were en-route to the neutral port of Barcelona. There this particular group of allied prisoners, destined for India, Australia and New Zealand, would be exchanged for Germans held in the Middle East and Egypt. Two other prisoner exchanges had already taken place a few days earlier. At Gothenburg, Germans, held in the United Kingdom and Canada, had been exchanged for prisoners from Britain, North America and South Africa. While the return of Germans held in Tunisia had taken place at Oran. News of the exchanges of 4,000 British and Empire prisoners and nearly 5,000 German prisoners was reported around the world. In Marseille, my father's contingent awaited the arrival of two boats that would take them to Barcelona for the third and final part of this exchange agreement.

Sunday, 24 October 1943 – Slept in until 8.30am. Beautiful weather again. Walked up to the Lazarett to collect our rations. The area was residential. Houses were quite modern… Later in the day we contacted French civilians under cover of the trees in the far corner of the grounds out of sight of the German guards. These people were very friendly passing bottles of wine and apples. Unfortunately one of the lads was spotted by the Jerries who set up a search. They then locked us in. During the evening (our last in Marseilles) beer and wine was brought in. German beer manufactured in Bremen specially for export. Quite good stuff. The wine was French… We are all packed ready to embark in the morning.

25 October 1943 – Called at 4.30am to find a gale blowing. Breakfast of acorn coffee and bread with cheese. Ambulances arrived at 6.00am. Passed down through the main street of Marseilles. Still raining. I was not impressed with the city, not that I saw much of it to form an opinion. Perhaps it was the dreary weather. Anyway duly boarded the boat—a former Italian hospital ship 'Aquileia'. Pretty ancient tub and doesn't look as though it will see the war out. The crew are mostly Italian with German Officers. We are in a long crowded ward – 100 of us. Toilet facilities are very primitive. Food rations are fair. Later on in the afternoon she started to rock and some of the lads were a little seedy. I felt quite OK. The old bus will only do 5 or 6 knots and is hugging the coast. Proceeding fully lighted. Should arrive in Barcelona at 6pm tomorrow.

As my father's boat steamed towards Barcelona, two boatloads of German POWs were making their way to Barcelona from Alexandria. One of the Germans on board was U-Boat ace Victor Oehrn. A Fregattenkapitan with the Kriegsmarine, Oehrn was credited with sinking twenty-four ships and had been awarded the Knights Cross. During a mission to North Africa in July 1942 a badly wounded Oehrn had been captured and taken to a British Military Hospital in Alexandria, before being transferred to POW Camp 306 on the Suez

Canal. Now, having been deemed eligible for repatriation, Oehrn and his compatriots on the British ships, HMSS *Tairea* and HMT *Cuba*, were headed for an unusual rendezvous of sorts with my father and his Empire companions on the German ships, *Aquileia* and *Djenne*.

* * *

Sailing along in sight of land, the *Aquileia* passed the coastal border station mid-morning. My father realised it must be Spain they were looking at now. On the horizon he admired the snow-capped peaks of the Pyrenees. At dusk, he thrilled at the sight of twinkling clusters of lights dotting the Spanish coastline, where no blackout was in force. It had been years since he had seen homes illuminated at night. He spontaneously burst into the Vera Lynn song, *When the lights go on again*. Freedom was in sight, and it felt great. There was a cluster of lights much bigger than the others far off in the distance. As they drew nearer, it proved to be Barcelona. They berthed at midnight. Before retiring to their beds on board, they were reportedly given an arrival message from the British Ambassador, Sir Samuel Hoare:

> *Their Majesties wish me to say how delighted they are that the days of your captivity are over, and that you are now on your way home. Their Majesties deeply sympathize with you in the sufferings you have endured, and are deeply grateful for the services you have rendered to the Empire.*

At last the day of the prisoner exchange dawned: 27 October 1943. My father woke bright and early and went out on deck to view Barcelona in the light of day. He observed the nearby docks arranged in blocks and thought they seemed rather complicated. Surveying the 360-degree panorama, he thought the city looked spectacular. Straight in front of them sprawled La Barceloneta. Stuck on the ship, he could only imagine what life might be like in the many barrios crammed below the cloudy skyline. Behind them an aerial cable car crossed the harbour. From the port side of the ship, he could see the tall, iconic monument of Christopher Columbus with arms outstretched pointing to lands across the sea. He thought of his land across the sea, the land of the long white cloud, and returning there very soon. It was beginning to sink in that going home might not just be a dream. My father headed inside. It was time to get ready before the official proceedings commenced.

Moored on the city-side of the extra wide wharf were the *Cuba* and *Tairea* carrying Victor Oerhn and his German colleagues. Wearing peak caps from the Africa campaign, locals had heard them singing as they came in to moor two days earlier. The two British ships, still housing the Germans, were almost a mirror image of the two German boats lined up on opposite sides of the wharf. Soon the prisoners would swap boats. Today this wharf, in the centre of the Port Vell area, houses the Maremagnum shopping mall and a large aquarium. Most people who enjoy these attractions today probably have no idea of the historic humanitarian exchange that took place right there during the Second World War. Though at the time, the people of Barcelona were rightly proud that their port was being used for a prisoner exchange. Peaceful Barcelona harbour provided the ideal frame for a safe exchange between the warring sides.

As the hour for the event drew close, local Spaniards began to line the port. Some planned to shower the prisoners with local delicacies such as almonds, oranges, nougat and sherry. Dignitaries began to arrive. Overseeing the operations were Sir Samuel Hoare and his German counterpart. In attendance were delegates from the International Red Cross, Spanish politicians, General Moscardo and wives of the VIP's. An atmosphere of anticipation and excitement filled the port of Barcelona as the POWs prepared to disembark their ships. Students from local German schools hovered nearby waving white handkerchiefs. In the middle of the wharf, among a collection of buildings, Spanish nurses waited. Dressed all in white, they stood in a line beside a long row of empty stretchers. With a folded blanket on each, the stretchers were about to be put to good use.

The first Empire soldier carried ashore was an Australian who had been captured in Libya. As his stretcher touched down on Spanish soil, his first remark was, 'Thank God'. Helped by members of the Spanish Red Cross, the 1,083 men aboard the *Aquileia* and *Djenne*, including Australians, Indians, Palestinians and 383 New Zealanders, began to disembark one by one. Men still waiting their turn peered hopefully through portholes in anticipation of their freedom. At the same time, on the other side of the wharf, the Cuba and Tairea began offloading their 1,061 German prisoners. Stretcher cases were carried off first and placed in a line along the ground. The German ambassador's wife gave the smiling German prisoners a bag containing handkerchiefs, wine, oil and dried fruit. The Civil Governor of Barcelona had a parcel ready and waiting for every prisoner, British and German. Each bag generously contained sugar, coffee, rice and chocolate – commodities that were in short supply.

Once everyone was off the boats they lined up on their respective sides of the wharf. The emotion of the moment was reflected in every single face. On the Empire side, Sir Samuel Hoare and Lady Maud spoke informally to the mostly Australian and New Zealand men as they waited in lines to walk to the British ships that would take them on to Egypt. Men with mutilated arms and legs smiled as cigarettes were lit and placed in their mouths. Following a roll call, the newly freed men were taken to their respective ships. Some shouted and sang with heart-warming joy. Returned from captivity, they were suddenly and miraculously free.

Journalists who were present spoke to some of the men and filed stories describing the extraordinary scenes as the prisoner exchange unfolded. One article in Adelaide's *The Advertiser* reported that the men seemed in good spirits, especially when they met Australian and

New Zealand nurses on their ship: '"Darling, you are the handsomest and loveliest being I have ever seen. Kiss me quick," said an Australian lance corporal to a middle-aged and motherly Australian nurse who met his stretcher on the gangway.' There was reportedly a lot more banter between the Empire men and nurses than there was amongst the more serious Germans. Only a well-disciplined burst of singing inside their new ship was heard from time to time.

My father talked occasionally about this momentous day in Barcelona. He never forgot having seen the Christopher Columbus monument from his boat. When I visited the city many decades later, seeing the Christopher Columbus monument was a bittersweet experience. While it was extraordinary to imagine that my father had seen the monument from his ship as he prepared to be exchanged in 1943, it was a poignant moment too. I knew that he never had the pleasure of going beyond the wharf and experiencing the unique city of Barcelona. More than once he told me about his surprise at the behaviour of the German soldiers that day.

'As we passed the Germans on the wharf, they raised their right arms defiantly, and chanted 'Heil Hitler',' he said, still sounding perplexed. He remained taken aback by their display of undying loyalty in saluting the Nazi Fuhrer, given that the tide of the war had begun to turn against them. His diary entry that day helped me picture this extraordinary moment in his life, a day where history was made as the first groups of POWs from Germany were repatriated. What good fortune my father had to be among them.

27 October 1943 – Reveille at 06:00hours. Disembarkation began at 09:00 hours with a great array of Spanish Red Cross orderlies, sisters, army officials and international delegates. As our stretcher cases went off so the German equivalent came on. Spanish Sisters were flustering around anxious to help carry luggage etc. Most of them were young and attractive. At last the walking cases left the ship. The great moment 'no longer in enemy hands' as I set foot on Spanish soil. I realise that it is not just a dream but reality. Then a pretty little Spanish nurse takes my kit bag and carries it over to the English ship. She told me she had been in Russia with the 'Blue Division' and even had a medal to show. She knew no English but spoke German. We saw the Germans crossing to the ship we had left. A fair number of amputations among them. They looked well fed.

Soon we boarded the ship. Received gifts from Red Cross – pyjamas, toiletries etc. An 8lb food parcel from the Spanish people of Barcelona – a kindly gesture also a basket of fruit – grapes, apples, bananas, oranges and pomegranates. They were marvellous. I had forgotten what a banana tasted like.

Installed in comfortable quarters. Dinner of steak and onions – yes real steak and real onions. Read up the recent events, war news etc. in the latest magazines available on ship. For the first time for many a long day 'The BBC news'. All the news is good. Although it seems that going on the German news we used to receive as POWs, the Germans are admitting the true state of affairs and are fairly up to date.

Once again welcomed by Ambassadors etc. on behalf of the Majesties. The Royal New Zealand Army Medical Corps are altogether in a Red Cross ship, berthed directly behind us. Roast mutton etc. comprised the evening meal. It's been a very full day and a very happy one with even happier to come. Longing to get home now. There is some talk of an optional trip to England but its home sweet home for me just as soon as possible. Lights out 21:30 hours.

The next day, aboard their new boats, the free men prepared to sail out of Barcelona. The ships that now contained the Germans were still moored on one side of the dock and the British vessels were on the other side, with long sheds between them. My father and his fellow repatriates had a good view of the former guests of the Allies as they departed first, bound for the Reich. A small group of Nazis from

Barcelona valiantly saluted Hitler prior to their departure, but they formed a lonely party on their side of the wharf. It was a completely different story on my father's side of the wharf. Half of Barcelona seemed to have turned out to cheer the Empire soldiers and many 'Viva Churchill' signs were chalked on wharf sheds.

As their ship began to move past the cheering crowds who lined the shore, the Spanish locals waved at the repatriated prisoners who crowded the decks, many with their wounds of war on display. There were men on crutches or propped up in hospital beds. Some had lost arms or legs. Many were skeletally thin. Among the bandaged men, some had white strips covering their eyes. It was heart-breaking to see the marks of war permanently stamped on such young men. But for now, seeming not to have a care in the world, these courageous men waved and sang as they sailed out of Barcelona. While hooters sounded across the harbour, I imagine some of the locals would have been overcome with emotion as these brave men – some maimed and irreversibly broken – sailed past. For my father, the day they sailed out of beautiful Barcelona harbour was unforgettable.

October 28 1943 – Back into 'army living' again. Morning tea at 06:30 hours. Breakfast at 08:00 hours, porridge, fish and potatoes. Inspection at 10:00 hours. The tugs tied on and began our departure from Barcelona. There were quite a number of Spanish people on the docks and as we moved further out a number of ships lay along the docks. People crowded the stern of each ship shouting, waving, clapping and finally cheering us. One of the ships had 'Vive la Churchill' chalked on the side. Altogether it was surprising demonstration. In the early morning mist little was to be seen of the city and soon sunny Spain was just a smudge on the horizon. Shortly afterwards we caught up with the ship containing the protected personnel. Now we are steaming side by side. I felt a little squeamish in the afternoon but recovered in time for tea. The sea became quite choppy about midday. Several of the lads are off colour. Heard the BBC once again. We have a six-day journey to Alexandria and pass through the straits of Sicily. Proceeding fully lighted, likewise the accompanying ship.

With the exchange in Barcelona completed, the selected Allied POWs had all now been safely delivered from Germany. Some were arriving back home in England, while others, like my father, had a longer homeward journey ahead of them. In an extraordinary coincidence, two of these repatriated men – my father and British soldier, Gaythorne Templer – would (seventy years later) have 6-year old grandchildren in the same year 1 class at Russell Lea Infant School in Sydney, Australia. Company Quartermaster Sergeant Templer had been captured in Abbeville in May 1940 and incarcerated in Nazi Germany for three and a half years prior to his repatriation. My father and Gaythorne would never know each other, but two of their grandchildren would become friends in Sydney in 2014.

* * *

Having left Barcelona behind, the *Tairea* pointed her nose in a south-easterly direction and the men settled back for the Mediterranean leg of their journey.

29 October 1943 – Weather has calmed down and the 'Tairea' has scarcely any motion at all. This boat is chiefly an Indian hospital ship, most of the crew are Indian. However there is a Sister to each ward. They are doing a fine job. Despite the fact that all the ships are protected, occasionally they are sunk. Quite recently the sister ship to this was sunk off Salerno! (Italy) While both ships were engaged recovering the wounded from the beach they were dive-bombed by German aircraft and the sister ship received a direct hit and was sunk. Fighting such a ruthless enemy, British Sisters take a considerable risk.

Today we collected £2 Egyptian currency. Received clothing issue, also beer and cigars (not much use to a non-smoker) and grapes as well. The two ships are still sailing merrily along side-by-side doing about 11 knots. Community sing song on deck. According to the news, Russians are sorting the Hun.

30 October 1943 – Sleeping like a top. Weather calm. Spent most of day dozing and reading in the extremely warm Mediterranean sun. Today we saw plenty of British aircraft and lots of small islands, passing quite close to Pantelleria, a rocky, barren place with a large green plateau near the summit, which is no doubt the aerodrome. 'Housie Housie' on deck.

Sunday 31 October 1943 – Day dawned bright and clear. Early morning saw a small convoy pass quite close escorted by a destroyer. Also sighted several more aircraft. Recognised a Bristol Beaufort! Late afternoon a squall struck with sudden fury, whipping up a comparatively calm sea into turbulent waves. This persisted and it looks like being a stormy night. I think I shall enjoy it as I have my 'sea legs' now.

Attended a divine service, a thanksgiving service as well it might be. How well I realise that. Plenty of fruit, beer and wine. Retired early.

1 November 1943 – Last night was rather rough with a high wind and the ship rocked a good deal. Consequently many of the lads were suffering from 'mal de mer'. At breakfast our table was depleted from 16 to 8, then rather hurriedly to 6, the smell of the food being the cause. It had its good points though as we who remained fit received double rations. Shortly after dinner the storm blew itself out. However I enjoyed it as I like to see the elements raging. A free issue of beer, wine and brandy served to make the evening pretty merry. Sighted land on the starb, probably between Benghazi and Derna. There was an Indian concert mostly in Hindustani. Have sent a cable home.

2 November 1943 – One of those beautiful wild sunny days. I spent the greater part of it right up on the bow, basking in the sun and a deliciously cool breeze watching the blue water. I think this weather is worth all the storms put together and if there is weather to be found in heaven, this must be it. No land in sight but I believe we berth at Alexandria tomorrow at 8am. We overtook another hospital ship during the evening. It's believed to be carrying wounded from Italy. Calm, starry night.

The delight of being free and homeward bound breathes in my father's diary entries. Comments such as, 'if there is weather to be found in heaven, this must be it,' provide a glimpse into his jubilant state of mind. I doubt he had ever felt so alive.

Six days after leaving Barcelona, Alexandria loomed on the horizon. Arriving in the harbour, they anchored well out from the dock, waiting while a large outward-bound convoy departed. My father was captivated by the passing parade of ships with large numbers of troops aboard. He counted about thirty ships in all, including destroyers, cruisers, battleships and water torpedo boats. *God help any sub that ever approached Alexandria.* As they got closer to the city, he observed that it was seething with life and activity. He turned up his nose as some strong aromas assailed him. Local kids roamed the port shouting 'Bucksheesh Mister' as they weaved their way through the throngs of people.

Early afternoon, with the aid of tugs, the *Tairea* threaded its way into the dock. Cheers could be heard around Alexandria harbour as locals tied the ship to the wharf near the Red Cross train that awaited them. The mayor and a large number of officials were there ready to greet the men. Medical staff hovered near the waiting refreshment wagon. The men filed down the gangway dressed in the khaki uniforms they had been given on the voyage, carrying their belongings in oddly assorted packages.

According to the NZEF Official War Correspondent, 'The sunshine of a typical autumn day was no brighter than the smiles and sallies of 383 New Zealanders – first to be repatriated from Germany – who disembarked today from the protected ship *Cuba* and the hospital ship *Tairea* after a six-day trip from Barcelona.' As they disembarked, cigarettes were handed around and British Red Cross girls surrounded the men, eager to do anything they could to help. All in all, my father thought it was a rousing welcome.

One girl dressed in white, with a Red Cross 'R' embroidered on her pocket, said to him, 'It's nice to have you back.'

'It's nice to be back,' he replied, smiling broadly.

The men trudged along the quay and boarded the Red Cross train that sat in readiness on the docks. As my father and some of the other repatriates stood looking out the carriage windows during the brief interval before they departed for Cairo, a New Zealand Army photographer took a photo of them. Over seventy years later, I happened upon the picture online. Zooming in on my father, nothing could have prepared me for seeing how he looked that day. Even knowing the hardship he had endured in Nazi Germany, I could never have come close to imagining what nearly two years as a prisoner of war had done to him. He was painfully thin, his gaunt face and sunken cheeks reminiscent of how he had looked as an old man. Even though he had told me that he'd been hungry for nearly two years as a POW, I'd never actually pictured him reduced to skin and bone, worn and haggard, an old man at 23. It took my breath away. I felt a profound sadness to see with my own eyes just how much he must have suffered.

Leaving Alexandria, they settled in for the eight-hour train journey to Cairo. My father opened the present from the Red Cross that awaited him on board. It contained a parcel of sweets and cigarettes, a bottle of beer, a newspaper, and a thoughtfully worded letter welcoming them back. The Kiwis also received a message from the New Zealand Government:

On behalf of the Government and people of New Zealand, I extend a warm welcome to you on your arrival in the Middle East and assure you that we look forward eagerly to your return to New Zealand. We know that those of your comrades who still remain in prison camps are bearing their trials with courage. Their early liberation will be secured by the victorious armies of the United Nations.

The men drank their beer and downed a satisfying supper before getting some rest in their sleeper carriages. Cairo was 'dead' when the train slowed on approach to the station at 2.00am. Peering out the window into the dark city, my father thought it looked 'pretty gruesome' and decided he wouldn't fancy wandering around on his own at night. After clamouring off the train, they were met by members of the New Zealand Medical Corps at the station; 169 sick or wounded New Zealanders were transferred to 1 NZ General Hospital at Helwan, a village eighteen miles up the Nile from Cairo. My father was delighted when he was directed to a big airy tent. He thought it was by far the best place to be in the desert heat. After drinking the soup and coffee that was brought around, he lay down in his tent in the middle of Egypt and closed his eyes. His brothers Ray and Keith had been posted to the Middle East with the New Zealand Army two years earlier and, as sleep overtook him, he wondered if they were nearby.

Chapter 15

'Land of the long white cloud'

But come ye back when summer's in the meadow.
Frederic Weatherly

For the next twenty days, my father was largely free to explore Cairo and its surrounds. Apart from having some administrative matters to take care of, he was officially on leave. Waking to bright sunshine and cloudless skies on his first morning at Helwan, he set off to stretch his legs and have a look around the Hospital Camp. His tent was located in a compound called 'Spencerfield' about two hundred yards from the main hospital building. It had formerly been a grand hotel and health resort where Kaiser Wilhelm reportedly spent his honeymoon, but now the crumbling three-storey building, with views of the Nile, was divided into wards for the war wounded.

My father looked out at the barren land around them. He batted away the flies that stuck to him despite his best efforts to discourage them. It reminded him of the way flies stick to cattle back home. He sighed. The sun was as hot as blazes. The heat, flies, ants and dust didn't hold any appeal. He perked up when ice creams were handed around. It had been a long time since he'd tasted ice cream and savouring every lick, he thought it tasted like nectar.

Venturing out of the compound to explore the local area, he hailed a *gharry*, as they termed the local horse drawn cabs. They clip-clopped slowly into town. After paying the driver, he hopped out onto the tree-lined main street. Browsing in the Helwan shops, he couldn't believe the prices. He decided things must have been marked up for the international soldiers based in the area: *I believe that since the war began there have been 500 millionaires created in this country.* His first impressions of Helwan left much to be desired: *I'm afraid I'm not going to like Egypt. Too hot, too dirty, too many flies, too dusty, too many smells and there's sand in everything. Still, I suppose I could get used to it if Ray could.*

The only thing he seemed to enjoy in his first few days in Egypt was swimming in the pool attached to the Kiwi Club. Half a mile from the hospital, on the outskirts of Helwan, was a club that was popular with New Zealanders based in the area. Set up by the Red Cross and run by the locals, the Kiwi Club was the place to while away the hours, relaxing on a comfy couch with a cup of tea and newspaper. Little touches, like the kiwi on the gate and the fresh flowers in the vases, gave the club a homely feel. Ping-pong and miniature golf were on offer for the slightly more energetic. My father always found someone interesting to chat with at the club.

Not long after arriving at Helwan, he was interrogated by an RAF officer. It was a very thorough process, involving several hours of questioning. The information he and the other repatriates provided was collated into a military intelligence report. Their comments were among the first eyewitness statements from prisoners in Germany and, as such, were highly valued. Medical and dental staff also interviewed him and provided inoculations and dental treatment.

One day he visited the RAF aerodrome in Helwan, where he acquired an Air Force uniform. A paymaster provided him with the money he was owed and he chose to donate some of it to the Red Cross. Nearly £2,000 was collected from the New Zealand repatriates and presented to the Red Cross in Cairo, such was their gratitude for the parcels that had kept them alive.

Once he had taken care of his official duties, he was keen to explore the big city of Cairo, but not before visiting Maadi Camp to enquire about his brothers. There, he spoke to a helpful person at 'Records' and learned that his eldest brother Ray was with the 24th Battalion while Keith was with the 4th Field Regiment. Both men were currently elsewhere with the New Zealand Division, so any reunion with family would have to wait.

While shopping in Cairo, my father bought some silk stockings for his mother and sisters, a bracelet for his niece, and a new watch for himself. Carrying his bags of shopping, he took the tram to the pyramids, and was awed by the Sphinx and temples. *Monstrous great things made out of huge slabs of stone. Well worth seeing. Standing alongside them and trying to imagine them being built 5,000 years ago gives one an idea of the minuteness of our own span of life.*

One evening he met some of the lads in town and went with them to a cabaret. It wasn't his scene at all: *I see nothing in such places. Anyway it's educated us in the ways of the world, but give me the open air, the open road, a cycle and let me ride away from the stigma of captivity and licentious living (must be feeling high minded).*

On 23 November, after spending nearly three weeks in Egypt, leave was suddenly cancelled for the day. At midday they learned that they were to be moved that evening. They boarded a Red Cross train at 10.00pm bound for Port Tewfik at Suez, arriving at the docks early the next morning. It could mean only one thing; they were about to board a boat that would take them on the last leg home. Disembarking the train at Suez, my father's eyes were drawn to a beautiful white ship moored apart from the other anchored vessels. Compared to their dreary wartime colours, her white hull sparkled. The vivid red crosses painted on her sides identified her as a hospital ship. I hope that's our ship, he thought. And it was. This grand, streamlined craft was scheduled to provide their passage to Australia and New Zealand. A former Dutch passenger liner, the MS *Oranje* had been converted to a hospital ship. My father couldn't wait to get on board and begin the final leg of their journey home.

24 November 1943 – This morning we are in Tewfik at the docks. We quickly dismounted the train and as the ship is out in 'stream' we went out in small lighters. Wasting no time at all we pulled alongside the 'Oranje' – up the gangway, given morning tea, then a beautiful berth. It's a clean hospital outfit with NZ sisters and nurses fussing about. The 'Oranje' did its maiden voyage two days after war broke out. It represents about the latest thing in hospital ships, very up to date, marvellous fittings and a fine second-class dining room for the patients. Capable of 30 knots, the journey to New Zealand will only take three weeks. Food is very good, everything is good. It's going to be a great trip home.

The stretcher patients were hoisted up by crane, two at a time. Once everybody was on board, final preparations for departure were completed. Before leaving the port at 4.00pm there was one last thing left to do: play the Maori farewell song, *Now is the hour*. An iconic song, that had been bidding New Zealand troops farewell since the First World War, it had become part of the national fabric. Everyone stopped what they were doing as the stirring tune began. Sung in Maori and English, the New Zealanders aboard all joined in, all the while daydreaming about their families back home who would be waiting while they sailed across the seas, closer and closer to reunion. And this long-awaited moment was now only three short weeks away. With their final journey underway, my father was overjoyed: *Homeward bound at last. It's a wonderful feeling. Hope I make it for Christmas dinner with the folks.* Oh what a Christmas it would be, perhaps his best ever. One thing was certain; it was going to be a big improvement on the Christmases of the past three years.

During the first few days of the voyage, the main topic of conversation amongst the men was the food. They couldn't get over how much there was to choose from or how delicious everything tasted, especially the ice cream.

November 24, 1943 – The sun is very hot and already I am taking
full advantage of it by spending most of the day 'browning off.' Meals
are excellent. Plenty of meat, vegetables, beautiful white bread, fruit
and ice cream. The Red Sea is just right at this time of the year. Also
the up-to-date air conditioning on this boat is perfect. Sleeping on top
of the sheets and doing it well.

After the rigours of war, travelling on the *Oranje* must have been
nothing short of extraordinary. The men could amuse themselves in
the sparkling swimming pool or play games on any of the eight decks.
Many thought the *Oranje* was the most beautiful ship they had ever
seen. 200 metres long and 25.5 metres wide, the *Oranje's* unique hull,
with a flared cut away bow, made her one the fastest motor liners of its
time. Many ships were left in her wake as they sailed down the Gulf of
Suez, across the Red Sea and into the Gulf of Aden.

Chatting to the crew, the patients learned that the *Oranje* had a
notable history. The Germans had invaded the Netherlands during
its maiden voyage in 1939, and ordered the captain to return to the
Netherlands. The captain had refused and the ship had subsequently
sailed to Australia where it was converted to a hospital ship at
Cockatoo Island Dockyards in Sydney. Remarkably, the *Oranje* had
left Sydney Harbour on 31 May 1942, one hour before three Japanese
midget submarines entered. Within hours one had attacked the HMS
Kuttabul, killing twenty-one sailors. Unbeknown to the crew of the
Oranje, but noted by the Japanese in their logs, the *Oranje* had passed
very close to the enemy submarines.

It wasn't just the ship that had an interesting past. Men with every
conceivable type of war experience were journeying home to Australia
and New Zealand. Along with the repatriated prisoners, there were a
large number of sick and wounded soldiers who had been in battles in
the Middle East campaigns. Some men had been wounded from as far
back as the Battle of Greece. There was no shortage of tales to tell as

they whiled away the hours, soothed by the gentle rocking of the deep, aquamarine sea.

27 November 1943 – Sailing up the Gulf of Aden today, almost due east. Passed several ships including another hospital ship. We simply leave them standing. More sunbathing. Am getting very red faced. Keeping fit on deck tennis. My muscles are sore from lack of use. We hear some very good musical 'medicine' from the ship's own records.

Along the vast Indian Ocean they sailed, across the equator, heading towards Australia. Sunshine and exercise was just what my father needed after languishing for so long in a miserable POW Camp. By the time the *Oranje* reached Melbourne in early December 1943, he was tanned and fit. Arrival of the repatriated POWs in Australia was reported in newspapers across the country. One article described the mixed feelings that were evident as the repatriated men were reunited with family members: 'Joy of reunion in some cases and sadness for misfortune in others were apparent in embraces. Some men met their children for the first time.'

After offloading the Australian soldiers, the floating hospital continued on towards New Zealand. My father's circumnavigation of the globe was almost complete. Up on deck on 14 December 1943, surrounded by the indigo waters of the Tasman Sea, his insides suddenly lurched with excitement. Below the huge gathering mass of clouds on the horizon, Aotearoa, the land of the long white cloud, was finally in sight. He stared longingly at his beloved New Zealand as they inched towards terra firma and the beautiful blur on the horizon slowly came into focus.

As they sailed into Wellington Harbour, he reflected on the tumultuous journey that had almost come to an end. It hadn't exactly been the 'great adventure' the happy-go-lucky 20-year-old had anticipated almost four years earlier when he'd left New Zealand.

What at times had been a 'ghastly nightmare' had been an enlightening journey nonetheless. Having completely circled the globe he had gained a wisdom that belied his young age. The many and varied experiences – some highly traumatic – would stay with him for life, shaping him for better and for worse. He thought of his mates Ian 'Robby' Robinson, Les Russell, and Robert 'Mac' McChesney, who had stood with him on the deck of the *SS Akaroa* watching New Zealand recede as they sailed to war in 1940. His friends would never see New Zealand again. Unlike so many, my father had made it home, against all odds.

I can only imagine his euphoria as he stepped off the boat in Wellington onto New Zealand soil again. I picture him pausing for a moment to fill his lungs with the fresh, clean, crisp, New Zealand air that signals to all intrepid Kiwis, they are home. As the large group of New Zealand soldiers disembarked, I imagine some of them might even have bent down to kiss the ground, their elation on display for all to see.

Before taking a train to Auckland the following day, my father attended a welcome home ceremony. Speaking on behalf of the Government, the Minster of Supply said how they appreciated to the very utmost what the returned men and women had done in this great struggle. 'You have played a part worthy of your country and worthy of our highest traditions, and we wish you every happiness in the future.' The Minister in Charge of Rehabilitation said he knew just how they all felt on returning home, and how good New Zealand looked to them, and he hoped that their homecoming would measure up to their long anticipation on the voyage home. For most of them, he said, their active service was over, but there was a lot still to be done, and everything possible would be done to help them take up where they left off. 'Whatever work you do your greatest and proudest memory will be that you have been members of New Zealand's Fighting Forces,' added the Mayor of Wellington, in his welcome on behalf of the city.

My father was also officially welcomed home by the RNZAF. Along with David Allen and Hugh English, he was amongst the first three

New Zealand airmen to be repatriated from Germany. The men would soon learn that they had been promoted to the rank of Warrant Officer while in captivity. Air Secretary Barrow and Air Vice Marshall Isitt formally welcomed the three men home, posing beside them for a photo for the newspapers. It was more than a month since my father had been photographed on the train in Alexandria, and I was relieved to see that he now appeared young and healthy once more. The hearty meals and rejuvenating sunshine on board the *Oranje* must have been just the tonic he'd needed. A newspaper article about the three repatriated airmen noted that one of them had gained two stone in weight since leaving Germany.

Arriving in Auckland a day later, the men were met by the Mayor and representatives of the Sick and Wounded Office. Red Cross transport cars were lined up ready to take them to their homes. The magical moment my father was anticipating had almost arrived. And it was going to be a glorious surprise for dad's family, who were not aware that he had arrived back in the country.

In a bay villa in Malvern Road, Mt Albert, dad's mother, the woman who would become my nana, was getting on with her daily chores. Unexpectedly, there was a knock at the door. Wondering whom it might be, she paused as her daughter-in-law walked along the central hallway to the door and opened it. Hearing some excited shrieking, she quickly made her way towards the front door. Standing right in front of her, dressed in his RAF uniform, was her son Ian, back from the war. She could scarcely believe her eyes. Great scenes of jubilation followed as other members of the family quickly joined them. When I was growing up, my nana told me of her surprise and delight at finding dad standing at the door, home from the war. I sensed it had been one of the greatest thrills of her life. Dad's youngest sister Mary remembered receiving an urgent phone call at work telling her to hurry home. Her brother was back from the war. My father had the reunion of a lifetime as his family and friends excitedly joined the celebration. Everyone was keen to hear whatever he was prepared to share about his odyssey. Back home in the family villa, he had never felt so happy to be exactly where he was. Of course he would never again be the innocent, idealistic lad who had volunteered to serve his country four years earlier. Forever changed, the Kiwi airman was home. As one of the lucky ones who had survived the war, he would get the chance to live beyond 23. He would have the opportunity to fall in love, get married and have children.

I would get to exist.

With only one week until Christmas, his arrival had given a great boost to the festivities in the Walker household. My father was quietly thrilled when he awoke on 25 December 1943 to have made it home in time for Christmas. The pohutukawa tree in the street was covered in a canopy of bright crimson flowers. There could be no better indication that it was Christmas in the place he called home. Knowing dad's luck, I'm sure he found a sixpence in his grandmother's Christmas pudding that year too.

Chapter 16

'The higher the fewer'

You cannot know the kindness of a man
Till you see him in a garden with a spade
And birds about his feet.

David Rowbotham

Even though my father was home, the war wasn't yet over. He often thought about his friends who were still POWs, and kept in touch with them. He received a postcard from his Canadian friend Larry Barjarow. Written on an official 'Kriegsgefangenenpost Postkarte' in 1944, Lance Corporal Barjarow wrote from Stalag IX-C Zweiglager:

Dear Ian
   Glad to get your letter. Everyone fine here. I'm in with the eye hospital. Just heard from Bill Watson, he is fine. Yes it must have been a great feeling to be free again and eat steak and onions. We are having rotten weather here now, cold and plenty of rain. Been in stalag here three weeks now. Quite a change from the other camp. All the best, Larry

Those who remained prisoners of war could only dream of eating steak and onions. With nothing better to hope for than a piece of potato in the so-called potato soup, Larry, like most POWs, would have to wait until 1945 before he would get anything more appetising. Larry's on-going incarceration highlighted just how fortunate my father was to have been plucked from his dire prison camp and returned safely to his privileged existence in the bottom corner of the world. Among the letters and news from the other side of the world, my father was sad to learn that Mrs Nicholl's house had been hit by a bomb. Despite the house being destroyed, she had survived, but then, after pining away in a rest home for a period, she passed away before the war's end.

Despite everything he had been through, I was astounded to learn that my father still wished to play his part in the war effort. I would have imagined he arrived home from the war mightily relieved, with no desire to return to the fray. On the contrary, according to his defence records, he informed the RNZAF that he would like to train as a pilot and resume duties in the Pacific. His passion to fight for freedom hadn't waned despite the emotional and physical scars he now carried. However he was advised that, according to international law as a repatriated prisoner of war, he was not allowed to undertake further combatant service. The RNZAF gave him the option of remaining with them as a gunnery instructor but he elected to take his discharge. Warrant Officer James Ian Bradley Walker officially left the service on 15 March 1944.

When the war finally ended in Europe in 1945, the British Air Council acknowledged 'the illustrious part which New Zealand airmen had played and the honour they had brought to their country and to the Royal Air Force by their gallant service in all theatres of war.' I'm sure my father's family felt justifiably proud.

* * *

Not long after arriving home from the war, my father and some mates went on a 500-mile cycle tour to the East Cape. It was great to be back on his bike after such a long time. Leaving Auckland behind, they cycled eighty-one miles to Paeroa on day one of their tour. It was the first long ride he had done for over four years and it tired him out. But he quickly got used to riding again. He was keen to resume bike racing once he got fit enough, and longed to regain his previous winning form. I wonder how it felt to finally 'ride away from the stigma of captivity' as he had dreamed over the past few 'weary years'. He marvelled at the pristine New Zealand scenery as he pedalled along. Having been around the world he saw it with new eyes, describing it affectionately in his cycle tours diary. Anyone who has returned home to New Zealand after a stint away knows just how breathtaking the country looks. How much more so after being locked up, only able to peer at the outside world through layers of barbed wire.

The scenery was great with towering, bush-clad cliffs rising sheer. Wild and rugged grandeur with many glades of fern and punga, cascading waterfalls of white ribbon, while far below the river foaming on its way made scenery second to none.

In time, my father had to try and settle back into a more normal existence and pick up the threads of civilian life. It was no mean feat after everything he had been through. He always said his former work at the butcher's shop held no appeal after the gory, gruesome things he had witnessed. Instead he chose to take on an apprenticeship in furniture upholstery. Three years after returning from the war, he met his wife to be, my mother Dorothy. I was born twenty years later with a lucky double crown (just like my father), the second of two girls. Like most young kids, I thought life began when I was born. My father was just 'dad': dad, the man who adored taking us on picnics, who played 'chasey' with us on the beach, who loved to spend every spare hour in his garden. He certainly wasn't dad, the war veteran to me.

For someone who had left school at 13 to help the family make ends meet, dad was surprisingly learned. Like many of his generation, he had grown up during the Great Depression and then gone to war. Life was the classroom and the lessons were challenging. When people ask me about my father, I describe him as someone who thought outside the square, and marched to the beat of his own drum. As a father, he was warm, wise, kind and nimble. I think the time he got to just sit and think as a POW had a lot to do with shaping the man I knew. I'll never know how different he would have been if he hadn't gone to war, but I suspect his war experiences had a profound effect on him. His deep-thinking, serious, and contemplative nature may well have been borne out of his long period of incarceration. Dad had a favourite joke he would trot out on occasion. It's an odd joke, but it sums him up rather well. When it was his turn to tell a joke, he would say somewhat formally, 'Why is a mouse when it spins?'

No one ever knew how to respond. Then he would say after a few moments of puzzled silence, 'Because the higher it flies the fewer,' followed by uproarious laughter, though it was invariably only ever dad who would be laughing. No one had a clue what he was on about. For some reason though, this joke appealed enormously to him. I never found anyone else who found it hilarious except him. Apparently Second World War soldiers sometimes used anti-humour jokes to identify Allies. Perhaps dad first heard his favourite joke during his time in the RAF. I can now see that so much of who my father was as a person, was shaped by his time at war. I'll always picture him tirelessly tending to his garden, with birds about his feet. Almost seeming to morph into the resident garden gnome, he seemed to spend every spare hour weeding, watering, pruning, planting and filling up his beloved bird bath. There was nowhere he would rather be than in the great, unenclosed outdoors. The garden was his passion and his joy and, perhaps, his therapy.

Having endured terrifying night raids holed up in a rear turret and been subjected to appalling treatment as a POW, it's hardly surprising that my father was affected psychologically. After the war in the 1940's, there was no psychological support available for those in the service. Nor was there much of a climate for talking about feelings and emotions among his generation. Perhaps he wouldn't have wanted to talk about such things anyway, preferring to just try and forget. Whatever he was dealing with, he largely kept to himself.

My father experienced symptoms of Post Traumatic Stress Disorder (PTSD) intermittently during his life. Sleep disturbance and re-experiencing symptoms, such as flashbacks and nightmares, were things he had to try and live with. The explanation a doctor gave him in the late 1940's for what he sometimes experienced at night was 'claustrophobia'. Dad first started to suffer from PTSD symptoms, while he was stationed at RAF Marham. He experienced troubling, anxiety producing sensations in bed at night, accompanied by a feeling that the walls were closing in on him. He didn't understand what was going on, nor did he say a word to anybody about it. Who could blame him? Anybody who did risked being diagnosed with 'lacking moral fibre' at the time.

It's been said that trying to cure PTSD is like trying to cure a memory. The horrors my father experienced during the war left an indelible scar. Sometimes at night he would re-experience the horror. During an episode, he would get out of bed, put the light on and pace around, trying to calm down. The only person he eventually talked to about these troublesome symptoms was his wife. My mother was an extraordinarily loving and selfless woman. I have no doubt that she helped him enormously.

I was unaware these episodes were taking place through the thin walls at home when I was growing up. Though, while I was fairly oblivious to what my father had to deal with, I guess I always knew at some level that the war had probably affected him, assuming he would have been a happier and more well adjusted person if he hadn't had to endure such traumatic experiences earlier in his life. And he didn't just have to endure these things during the war; he had a lifetime of re-experiencing to endure. For many servicemen, their war didn't end on VE or VJ day. They continued to wage a silent war from which they could not return. I struggle to reconcile the lifelong difficulties so many war veterans experience. It seems too much to expect anyone to bear.

I glimpsed the makings of my father's claustrophobia the day I peered into the rear turret of the Wellington bomber on display at Brooklands Museum in London. I was unprepared for the surge of emotions I felt when I first saw the hulking great bomber, its 86 ft wingspan almost filling the cavernous hangar. Tacked onto the very end of the fuselage was the small, perspex and metal turret that had been my father's cave during the long, cold, dangerous hours of a bombing raid. The reality of what my father must have experienced became clearer to me. Picturing him in his turret in the midst of a raid, I was awestruck that he had been prepared to undertake these missions, and amazed that he'd found a way to navigate such a death-defying challenge, night after night.

Inexplicably I sensed something of my dad in that turret. Or was it that the turret had always been part of my father? I can't entirely explain what I sensed at the time. But in seeing the rear turret of a Wellington bomber, something about it seemed strangely familiar. It was a similar feeling to the one I'd had sorting through my father's possessions after he'd died. In handling items like his gardening hat, something of his essence had been there. It didn't entirely make sense to me but then when I thought about it, perhaps if he had spent most of his life trying to escape the psychological effects of being in a cramped turret during a raid, then perhaps the turret had always been a part of him. I had expected a gun turret and my father to be entirely incongruent, but they weren't. Perhaps he had never managed to free himself, entirely, from the confines of a turret. In the same way one might think of someone carrying a weight on their shoulders, perhaps sometimes he still felt encapsulated by an invisible turret.

My father sought ways to minimise the PTSD symptoms that bothered him throughout his life. Being an intelligent, self-reliant individual, he discovered that the fitter and healthier he was, the less he was affected. And so began a lifelong quest to be in tip-top health. Dad left no stone unturned in order to ensure he was in the best possible condition. He grew organic fruit and vegetables in the back garden, fifty years before it became fashionable, consuming large quantities of them everyday. He was an early adopter of the jogging craze, and kept extraordinarily active his entire life. He ate homemade, stoneground, wholemeal bread, eschewed alcohol and became a vegetarian. He meditated and explored matters spiritual and philosophical, in an attempt to make sense of the unexplainable, finding great insight in the writings of Austrian philosopher Rudolf Steiner. As well as helping him cope with his PTSD symptoms, my father's strategies for healthy living and his devout spiritual beliefs stood him in good stead. He was a walking testament to everything he believed in, enjoying excellent physical health throughout his life. He scarcely needed to visit a doctor and didn't require any regular medication even in the final stages of his life. Despite the trauma he had endured, he developed an extraordinary resilience. Somehow he weathered a formidable storm, and prevailed.

When he was alive I never knew exactly why he was so consumed with being healthy, but I did marvel at how ahead of his time he was. Today it isn't unusual to eat organic vegetables and wholemeal bread, but back in the 1960s and 1970s in New Zealand, it was virtually unheard of. After dad passed away, I came across something he had written which said that he had been able to reduce his claustrophobia by being in optimal health. I had never known that was the reason he took such an extreme approach to healthy living. It explained a lot. I also discovered it was why he had absolutely refused to wear a seat belt while driving. Claustrophobia made him averse to being strapped into anything. He would stringently avoid confined places. Even in his eighties he elected not to go on the tubes in London for this very reason.

Dad opened up ever so slightly about what he would quietly refer to as 'my claustrophobia' in the final decade of his life. He shared a little with me about it, not much, but he certainly seemed more comfortable talking about it the older he got. Perhaps, as the end of his life loomed, he was more comfortable facing such challenges in ways not possible when much of life is yet to be navigated. I think it was also because of the changing times. He couldn't help but be influenced by the way we are more open about many things today. I remember him being highly impressed when former All Black Sir John Kirwan fronted a social marketing campaign to raise awareness about mental health issues. In it, Kirwan shared his personal experience of depression. At the time it was groundbreaking stuff. We all realised that if a legend like Kirwan could suffer from mental illness, anyone could. It seemed to me that the Kirwan campaign was a turning point for my father. It somehow gave him permission, towards the end of his life, to be able to share a little about the psychological challenges he lived with.

The psychological legacy of war that my father carried throughout his life wasn't all that obvious to the untrained eye. Nor would many have noticed the way the ankle of his injured leg often bothered him, affecting his gait almost imperceptibly. What was more apparent was his fixation on world affairs and impending doom. He seemed to spend his whole life expecting something dreadful might happen. I'm not sure exactly what he was expecting: World War III? Armageddon? After experiencing the might of the Nazis, maybe it wasn't too much of a stretch to imagine apocalypse. Having been witness to such atrocity, perhaps he could never naively expect world peace.

Dad was well versed with news and current affairs and would often have an interesting take on what he thought was *really* going on. Having become accustomed to the way the narrative was controlled during war, he continued to be sceptical about what he heard at times and relied on multiple sources of information to form his worldview. He would sometimes surprise you with the things he had to say. Like the time

I was staying at my parent's house on the morning of 12 September 2001, and woke them up early in the morning with the awful news that two planes had flown into the World Trade Centre.

'Goodness,' my 81-year-old father exclaimed in his groggy, only half-awake state, sheets still pulled all the way up to his nose.

And then straight away, with uncanny accuracy, 'That'll be Osama Bin Laden'.

I didn't ask him to elaborate at the time, but of course it turned out to indeed be the work of Bin Laden. Not much on the international stage escaped him. Having fought at the coalface of the Second World War, and followed its progress from within New Zealand, Britain and Germany, it makes sense to me now that dad enthusiastically continued to follow world affairs throughout his life. Having been prepared to give his life in the 'fight for freedom', as many of his mates tragically did, I now understand why the state of the world mattered so much to him. He cared deeply about the way the world is run and endeavoured to keep across developments all his life.

He passionately 'exercised his democratic rights' and took voting in an election extremely seriously. Having experienced the abuse of power first-hand in Nazi Germany, my father was only too well aware of the corrupting potential of power. He was always alert to the possibility of power being misused, decrying the lack of transparency and accountability too often associated with it. He expected a lot from the news media, mindful of the special role a robust, independent media play in a free and democratic society. It bothered him immensely when the media reported things in an unbalanced or manipulative way.

Those who knew my father couldn't help but notice his unconventional approach to many things. He was even committed to green, environmentally friendly living, long before it was widely acknowledged as essential to the future of the planet. For this, and so much more, he has long been an inspiration to me. On one particular occasion his inspiration proved particularly invaluable.

Chapter 17

'A dream that war had denied'

Made weak by time and fate, but strong in will
To strive, to seek, to find, and not to yield.

Alfred, Lord Tennyson

D ad had been overjoyed when he was fit enough to resume his competitive cycling career after the war. I remember him telling me, when I was growing up, that he had been very close to going to the Commonwealth Games, known as the Empire Games in his day. We were doing the dishes at the time. Dad would always wash, and I would dry.

'You know, I once won a trial race for the Commonwealth Games,' dad said with a hint of pride in his voice.

'Really?'

'Yes. But I only got fourth in the second trial.'

'You must have gotten very close to being selected.'

'Mmm'

'But the selectors didn't put you in the team?'

'No, my leg was never quite the same again after the war,' he said nonchalantly.

I don't think he ever wasted much time worrying about what could have been but, all the same, it must have been disappointing to get so tantalisingly close. He'd had to be content with sitting in the audience at the velodrome at the 1950 Empire Games in Auckland watching some of his cycling friends compete for New Zealand. Of course he would loved to have been racing, but he cheered with gusto for his mates.

Growing up, I was in no doubt that my parents loved sport. When the Olympics or Commonwealth Games were on every two years, the television was on non-stop. Lots of shouting and cheering would ensue. When I was very young, New Zealander Dick Tayler won the 10,000m at the 1974 Commonwealth Games in Christchurch. In a frequently replayed sequence, he famously leapt up and down before collapsing onto the ground, his joy and ecstasy on display for the world. My parents were almost as ecstatic, jumping up and down like crazy people. I think that day a little seed was sown deep within me. My own sporting dreams were ignited. For dad though, the war had meant he wouldn't get to wear the silver fern as an athlete. He had to be content with living vicariously through the likes of Dick Tayler.

Dad and I had a lot in common when it came to sport. Like him, I was a kid who dared to dream of going to the Olympics. It wasn't just some half-hearted notion. It was a dream that burned deep within me. I don't know why, but competing at the Olympic Games was something I dearly wanted to do from a young age. Somehow I just had to find a way to get there. Perhaps I had unknowingly been handed the Olympic torch and I would have done anything to keep the flame burning. My parents were wonderfully supportive of my sporting dreams. They provided all the support one could hope for, but were never at all pushy; simply doing anything they could to help because that was just the sort of people they were. It was fortunate for me, because in New Zealand there was no infrastructure or support to speak of for athletes from my chosen sport: gymnastics. The Australians had their world-class Institute of Sport. The impressive athletes from the 'Eastern Block' were the outcome of a system where developing champions was a national priority.

Perhaps naively, I didn't feel the significant hurdles in attempting to compete on the world stage were insurmountable. I was brought up with a notion that anything was possible. I found it helpful having a parent who had been a top athlete himself. Dad didn't get very involved in my gymnastics, but every now and then he would say something that indicated how well he understood what I was trying to do. Before leaving the house to go to a major competition, I'd go and say goodbye to my father. He would invariably look up from whatever he was doing and say, with a hint of optimism, '*Rise* to the occasion.' He never knew it, but I thought of his saying that, as my good luck charm. If he didn't say it, I'd hang around and make conversation until hopefully it occurred to him to say it. Perhaps I was hoping some of his legendary luck would rub off on me.

At various times in his life, my father seemed to have his own inbuilt, magical, lucky charm. He won numerous competitions over the years, such as the crossword competition in the local newspaper, which he won so often they asked him if he would stop entering. He was on the long-running New Zealand television game show *It's in the Bag* and won a significant amount of money. Most memorable of all was when he correctly guessed the cricket score of a one-day international and won several thousand dollars. It was a timely win too because we were struggling to fund my upcoming overseas gymnastics tour and it was a welcome relief to our fundraising efforts.

After more than a decade of dedicated training, I was on tenterhooks as I waited for the New Zealand Olympic team to be announced in 1988. In a strange twist of fate I had boarded a flight bound for a competition in Tokyo, two hours before the team was due to be announced on Radio New Zealand at 8.00pm. As I watched a movie on the Air New Zealand plane, 30,000 ft above the South China Sea, I checked my watch. It was a few minutes after 8.00pm. I realised my parents and friends would know by now whether I had made the team. I was by no means a certainty for selection. The New Zealand Olympic team selectors were notoriously tough, requiring athletes to have achieved very high world rankings. The movie dragged on as I tried not to ruminate about whether or not I had made the team. It was agonising to be up in the sky, unable to hear the news.

The movie finished and as the credits began to roll up the screen, a flight attendant tapped me on the shoulder. I hastily removed my headphones.

'Are you Angela Walker?' she asked.

I nodded.

'Would you like to follow me,' she said, motioning towards the front of the plane. 'The pilot has a message for you.'

Surprised, I stood up, my heart starting to race and followed her down the narrow aisle, up the stairway and into the cockpit. She introduced me to the pilots. It seemed as though the introductions took a lifetime as the moments ticked away before my fate would be revealed. Finally the pilot handed me a folded piece of paper. I opened it and read the fifteen words written on it: 'Angela Walker is the only gymnast to be selected for the New Zealand Olympic team.' I smiled and thanked the pilots, trying to contain the emotions bubbling inside. I wanted to jump and whoop, but I was in the confines of a 747 cockpit, surrounded by strangers. The flight attendant took me into first class and poured me a glass of champagne. It felt like a glorious dream.

When I think back on the unique circumstances surrounding my Olympic team selection, I can't help thinking how oddly fitting it was. The daughter of an Air Force man, whose war injuries had denied his sporting dreams, learns of her Olympic selection on a plane: on a plane bearing the Koru insignia on the tail. Sometimes life can be poetic.

Competing at the Olympics was an amazing life highlight. I was inspired by the ideals of the Olympic movement and the role it plays promoting international understanding and a peaceful world for all humanity. I proudly wore the silver fern and the interlocking Olympic rings, which symbolise peace among nations. Having had the experience of a lifetime at the Olympics in Seoul, South Korea, I was faced with a tough decision. Competing at the Olympic Games had always been my goal. Now I'd reached an age where gymnasts typically 'retired', and I felt ready to hang up my ribbon. Spending many hours of the day in a gymnasium, training hour after hour, held less appeal now that I had achieved my Olympic dream. Life outside of a gymnasium beckoned. However the Commonwealth Games were only fifteen months away and were to be held in my hometown of Auckland, and rhythmic gymnastics would be one of the sports contested for the first time in Commonwealth Games history. I had to decide whether to carry on training several hours a day for this major event.

I agonised for weeks over the decision. Knowing I was torn, my father asked me one day how I thought I might feel in just over a year, sitting in the audience watching the Games as a spectator. I knew in an instant that I had to keep training. And it was just as well I did because I had the good fortune to win a gold medal and three bronze. It's only when I look back on all of this that I realise my father was able to quietly guide me towards this achievement because he had known first-hand the disappointment of sitting in the audience at the Commonwealth Games in his hometown, wondering what could have been.

Without the extraordinary support of my mother and father, I could never have achieved my impossible dreams. No New Zealand rhythmic gymnast has won a Commonwealth Games medal or qualified for the Olympic Games since then, such is the challenge in a small country not resourced for high performance in this discipline. My father was an ordinary man who had done extraordinary things. Somehow I think the resilience and single-minded determination he developed during and after the Second World War played a part in creating an environment in which I could aim for the sky. It's not lost on me that I am one of the lucky ones. More often we hear tragic tales of suffering from children of war veterans. Intergenerational transmission of trauma is a deeply disturbing legacy of war. I am profoundly grateful that my father's influence on me, despite the traumas he endured, was overwhelmingly positive.

Standing on the dais at the 1990 Commonwealth Games, watching the New Zealand flag rise as my home crowd sung the national anthem, was a once in a lifetime experience. I imagine it must have been extraordinary for my father too, as he stood only metres away in the audience that evening. It was the second time the Commonwealth Games had been in Auckland and both times he had been a spectator. This time, he described it as one of his life's highlights. Perhaps it was a reward he received for the sacrifice he had made much earlier in his life. Dad was far too humble to have ever seen it like that, but regardless, I'm honoured that I could carry the torch and bring to fruition a dream that war had denied him.

* * *

Of course my father had already earned medals of incomparable value: war medals that are in a league of their own. Like many men of his generation, Ian Walker left his family who follow him, a remarkable legacy. I don't suppose he ever imagined, when he climbed into a plane night after night during the dark years of the war, that his involvement in the Battle of Britain would mark his name in the record books forever as one of a legendary 'Few'.

For most of his life, little attention was given to his wartime exploits by him or others. There were plenty of people who knew him, who would have had no idea that he was a decorated Second World War veteran. He rarely talked about himself and certainly didn't concern himself with what others thought. A favourite aphorism that he liked to trot out at pertinent times was: 'The world will little note nor long remember.' But all this changed in 2005 when he was invited to the sixty-fifth anniversary celebrations of the Battle of Britain. I had the privilege of accompanying him to a weeklong series of special events, held in honour of 'The Few' – the crewmembers of fighter aircraft who took part in the Battle of Britain during the period 10 July–31 October 1940. Dad was 85 at the time. High time the tables were turned and I was there to celebrate *his* achievements.

On Battle of Britain Day, we attended the 'Salute to the Few' dinner at Northolt Aerodrome. To begin the evening, three Spitfires roared overhead giving the veterans a dramatic flypast salute. It was a 'nostalgic moment' for dad and the other Battle of Britain airmen. Some of 'The Few', eighty in fact, were still fit enough to attend the event. While dad was being reacquainted with a group of colleagues he hadn't seen for a very long time, HRH Prince Philip, the Duke of Edinburgh, was led over to the group. Amid the introductions my father and the Duke shook hands.

'What squadron did you serve in?' the Duke asked him displaying a genuine interest.

'I was in 600 Squadron Your Royal Highness,' my father said with a natural formality.

'Ah, City of London Auxiliary Squadron.'

Dad nodded. 'Yes, that's right, we were based at Manston.'

'Where are you from?'

'I'm from New Zealand, Sir'

'New Zealand. Did you emigrate there after the war?'

'No, I was born there. I came to England with the RNZAF in 1940.'

'And were you a pilot?'

'I was an Air Gunner and Radar Operator.'

Someone managed to take a photo of this auspicious conversation. In it, dad, making a rare appearance in his suit, looked just the part with his Battle of Britain tie, and medals adorning his jacket. He seemed humbled by the presence of royalty and the formality of the occasion. It didn't seem to have occurred to him that he was one of the heroes we were there to honour.

Before long it was time to take our seats for dinner. There was one Battle of Britain veteran at each large, round table. Dad, our table's VIP, was seated next to the sister of a senior member of the Air League, who seemed almost overwhelmed to be sitting next to him. She told him what a great privilege it was to have been placed next to such a brave person and kept saying how honoured she felt, giving him several little hugs during the evening. Her thoughts were echoed by the others at the table. Dad whispered to me at one point, 'I think I'm being mistaken for someone else.' He didn't feel as though he was anybody particularly special. But everyone at the table clearly thought he was.

Before dinner was served, a hush came over the room and we all turned our attention to two large screens on the stage. Time was wound back to August 1940 and to Churchill making one of his famous speeches. It was the iconic speech that led to the Allied airmen of the battle ultimately becoming known as 'The Few'. Humbled by the bravery and sacrifice of 'The Few', I found it hard to believe my unassuming father was part of such an exalted group. After grace had been said, we dined on fine British cuisine, finishing with chocolate mousse adorned with a pastry Spitfire, before it was time for the speeches. The Duke of Edinburgh reminded us the odds were not in our favour during the Battle, and success was due to the extraordinary courage, endurance and tenacity of the men who fought in the skies for our freedom all those years ago. In defeating Germany for the first time during the Second World War, the Battle of Britain had become one of history's true turning points.

If dad wasn't already feeling overwhelmed by the sincere gratitude that had been expressed numerous times that evening, the final ceremony would do it. Each veteran was presented with a miniature Spitfire propeller with diamond inset, designed by Sarah Faberge. It was an emotional moment for dad, a gift he would treasure and an evening he would long remember. Dad had never expected to be so

212 Abbey From Battle of Britain Airman to POW Escapee

feted. But then, I don't suppose he had ever expected as a young man, he would play a part in one of the most critical battles of the war.

A few days later we attended a service at Westminster Abbey on Battle of Britain Sunday, to commemorate the sixty-fifth anniversary of this dramatic turning point in the Second World War. The day dawned crisp and sunny. Dressed in our finery, we lined up waiting to pass through the security checks at the entrance to the Abbey, but dad was quickly ushered straight through. After all he had done, it seemed fitting that he was deemed to be no threat. We sat solemnly for the duration of the service. Towards the end, the Dean of Westminster said, 'Almighty God, into your hands we commend the souls of those who laid down their lives for the cause of freedom.' I later learnt from my father's diary that he was silently paying tribute to all who died honourably in the service of their countries on both sides. That was very much who my father was.

As we waited our turn to be ushered out of the Abbey after the service, we sat lost in reflection while the musicians played Handel's Water Music. I knew it was one of my father's favourite pieces of music. What I didn't know was the intense and deeply personal emotions he had been feeling throughout this solemn ceremony. He didn't say anything at the time, but alluded to them in his trip diary.

September 2005 – A glorious cathedral with its stone pillars formed with incredible detail. The sheer height of ceiling defies logic as to how it was built. There were no cranes in the 12th Century. The beauty of it all, the intricate nature of design that gives such perfect acoustics in every part, the skill of the stonemasons that built it, albeit over a long period, calls forth the greatest admiration. Words cannot adequately describe Westminster Abbey. One has to see it for oneself.

Among our many highlights, Westminster Abbey must stand out as a solemn remembrance of those who made the ultimate sacrifice in laying down their lives in the cause of freedom. Poignant memories were

surging through my heart surrounded as we were by many another
with thoughts that run too deep for words.

With everything he had been through in the 1940s, I am not surprised that he had neither the will nor the words to express the river of emotions that ran so deep. Perhaps, as is said: 'great griefs are silent.' Yet sixty-five years on, he was no less clear about the reason he and his friends had been prepared to die. The cause of freedom was a cause he was, understandably, still just as passionate about.

After the service at Westminster Abbey, we were taken to Victoria Embankment beside the Thames for the unveiling of a magnificent monument that pays tribute to 'The Few'. Knowing it was probably the last opportunity to hold a reunion with such a large number of veterans, no effort was spared in making the sixty-fifth anniversary celebrations truly remarkable. Prince Charles unveiled the 25m long bronze sculpture depicting scenes from the Battle of Britain. On the outside, bronze plaques list the names of 2,936 allied airmen who took part in the Battle, above Sir Winston Churchill's immortal words: 'Never in the field of human conflict was so much owed by so many to so few.' It's a fitting tribute to the selfless commitment and determination of 'The Few' – the remarkable men who changed the course of history. And a proud day for my father as he got to see his name permanently etched into history in the great city of London.

After the pomp and ceremony of the official event, the public were allowed in to view the monument and mingle with the veterans. It was strange to see my humble father, from far off New Zealand, having people line up to get his autograph in central London. A retired upholsterer, happiest pottering in the garden, was suddenly in demand.

'You make me feel like a football star,' dad said to one young man as he signed his programme.

'You're worth *hundreds* of those Sir,' the man replied, his respect and gratitude almost palpable. I'm not sure if I realised it at the time, but this was a young man I had something to learn from.

That evening dad recorded the day's events:

Coaches took us to the Embankment for the unveiling by Prince Charles, with Camilla by his side. We were seated in a stand in the front row and had a good view. Prince Charles gave a fine speech before unveiling a most impressive monument much larger than I expected, along with sculpted figures in stone. Notable landmarks including St Paul's also adorned the sides. The names of all who took part engraved in bronze around the lower section, country by country—my own being in the New Zealand section. I found the names of my friends Les Russell, Ian McChesney.

After a reception in the Defence Headquarters we went back to more closely examine the monument. Lots of the public were also doing the same. I, with my medals on my chest, became a focus of attention and was asked to sign numerous books and programmes. The English even after all this time revere the so-called 'Few' and it seems that it will always be so.

At the time, while I did know how special the events I attended with my father were, I knew little of the memories or emotions he carried with him. I now appreciate how therapeutic it must have been for him to see his fallen friends' names permanently etched in stone, and to have his own contribution recognised. My father received due recognition for the part he played in the Battle of Britain. He was flown from New Zealand to London for commemoration events on three occasions in the final two decades of his life. His name is carved into monuments leaving an impressive legacy acknowledging his bravery during the Battle of Britain. But for his time in bombers – which for him, was a far more death-defying experience – he was never recognised.

There were no medals specifically awarded to the men from Bomber Command after the war. Winston Churchill failed to mention them in his victory speech, even though they were the service with the highest percentage of losses. It wasn't until 2012 that Britain finally officially honoured the men from Bomber Command, or until 2013 that veterans could apply for the newly created Bomber Command clasp, nearly seventy years after the end of the war. Why, then, did it take so long to recognise these men? Nearly half of the 125,000 airmen of Bomber Command were killed in action. No one could doubt that their sacrifice and contribution was immense. Towards the end of the war however, the intense bombing of German cities and the ensuing firestorms and mass civilian deaths made the bombing campaigns highly controversial. After the war it was more convenient to brush it all under the carpet. The passage of time seems to have enabled the bravery and sacrifice of those who served in Bomber Command to have finally been acknowledged. But in 2012, it was three years too late for my father. He had already passed away, as had most of the veterans who survived the war.

Chapter 18

'A giant wheel of destiny'

Shine through the gloom and point me to the skies.

Henry Francis Lyte

D ad died in his ninetieth year. He had remained fit and active until the end, thanks to the healthy lifestyle he had long adopted. 'Old age'– as the doctor wrote on his death certificate as the cause of death – had eventually caught up with him. In his last few days, dad seemed completely prepared for the end of his earthly life. Having cheated death time and time again during the war, and buried most of his friends and family over the course of a lifetime, he was strangely comfortable with death.

I tried to take some of his enthusiasm for a funeral with me the day I went to his. When it was my turn to stand in front of the gathered mourners and tell them about my father, there was so much I could have said: about a man who grew up during the Great Depression in peaceful New Zealand before he was thrust into the darkness of a world war; about a man who was a champion cyclist whose dreams were shattered along with his leg when his plane crashed in Nazi occupied Belgium; about a man who loved organic gardening and esoteric books. Looking out at the room full of friends and family dressed in black, I shared some of my treasured memories before concluding with the part of my father's life that had impressed me the most.

'Dad spent a great many years caring for mum as her health declined,' I said. 'His devotion and dedication to caring for her was *phenomenal*.' I glanced up and all eyes in the room were gently on me. 'In fact, of all of dad's achievements in life,' I said, 'it is for *this* that I am most proud.'

It was true. It seems incomprehensible to me now, but at the time, I was far more proud of the extraordinary way he had devoted himself to caring for my sick mother around the clock for years, than I was of all the war medals that sat in his sock drawer. War simply horrified me and I found it hard to feel proud of anything to do with it. I did wonder if I should have felt more proud of the way my father had bravely joined the fight against tyranny and oppression in the early 1940s, but, at the end of my father's life, I actually thought his extraordinary care of my mother had been his finest hour.

I managed to get through my speech without breaking down. To finish, I turned towards the coffin. 'Dad you were a wonderful man: deep, loving and wise, and I couldn't be more grateful that you were my father,' I said, the emotion welling up inside me, threatening to erupt. 'I'll miss you greatly, but I know you are at peace.'

I returned to my seat. My little boy gave me a squeeze, my husband a supportive smile. The piano began to play one of dad's favourite songs. We all joined in.

'Oh Danny Boy. The pipes the pipes are calling....'

The room resounded with the warm tones of the Irish melody. It felt as though the whole room was sending dad off with love. Then the coffin bearers solemnly carried the coffin down the aisle to the distinctive tones of the Last Post – a fitting tribute to a war veteran. He had even died on the sixty-fifth anniversary of D Day: 6 June 2009. Dad was gone, taking many of his Second World War experiences to the grave, and unknowingly, I was still the naïve girl with the poppy: highly idealistic and not very well appraised of my father's experiences.

My father came from a generation that has sometimes been described as the 'greatest generation'. It's not hard to see why. But I haven't always completely understood this. Without diminishing my respect for the way he cared for my mother so ardently in her final years, it is only now after discovering his diaries and piecing together his journey, that I realise his service during the war was in fact the most laudable aspect of his life. I am extraordinarily proud of the way he stepped up, with courage and determination, when the world was cast in an appalling darkness. How he ultimately became a wise and loving man, who touched the lives of those who knew him despite the traumas he'd suffered, is all the more remarkable. Anyone who was brave enough to take on the Nazis and fight for our freedom deserves my utmost respect and gratitude. But it wasn't until I had uncovered dad's wartime story and immersed myself in that period of history that I truly understood this. There's no doubt his journey around the world during the war was a journey of great enlightenment for him, influencing his whole life. Similarly for me, joining up the dots of his time at war has been an eye-opening journey. On countless occasions, I have been overcome with emotion as I pieced his story together and witnessed the enormity of the sacrifices made by those who serve.

I can't help feeling regret that I didn't better understand my father and his war experiences when he was alive, though perhaps it was for the best. Living in a house full of females, who didn't show a great deal of interest in his war, may have been just what he needed in order to move on and transcend the difficult memories. But I do wish I had fully appreciated and properly honoured the sacrifices he made. Much like the Bomber Command Memorial, my full appreciation didn't come until after my father was gone. To his credit, dad never sought nor needed recognition, simply describing himself as 'a small cog in a giant wheel of destiny.' Dad knew that he was merely one of many millions of people with a war story. Courage or suffering had not been in short supply amongst his peers and my father didn't think of his story as anything particularly special. Special or not, every story is worth preserving whenever possible. After all, the stories of so many airmen were only ever told in long gone vapour trails.

Why, though, did it take so long for me to recognise my father's finest hour? My strong anti-war feelings were the main cause. My lifetime to date has coincided with a period of history where, arguably, some dubious wars have been fought. During this time, I was greatly influenced by a man who had himself experienced the horror of war. Having witnessed its death and destruction first-hand, my father, like many returned servicemen, had little appetite for it. He knew the futility of war, and didn't necessarily see it as the answer to the challenges of the post-war era. He wanted me to know that war is a terrible thing. He brought me up to not always take things at face value, and to hope for a world where peace and tolerance are valued. My great aversion to war meant that, ironically, I didn't take a great interest in dad's experiences when he was alive. Knowing my father had suffered lifelong consequences of war was another major contributor to my anti-war feelings. It's hard to see someone you love, impacted for life.

In naively wishing there had never been a war, I hadn't entirely figured out that it is the oppressor who ultimately decides the nature of the conflict. The Allies were left no alternative in the end but to use some methods that mirrored the enemy. Pacifism is great in theory, but it wasn't much use when faced with the might of the Nazis. Neither had I figured out that I could commemorate war without actually celebrating it. I've come to realise, with the passage of time, that I can simultaneously honour the sacrifices of those who served the nation in wartime while not glorifying or eulogising war. We say, lest we forget, for so many reasons. We wish not to forget the price of war.

I think it's fair to say my father came to believe that war should absolutely be avoided if at all possible, but not at all costs. He did what had to be done and had no regrets about having done his duty, fighting to preserve freedom and democracy. (Though he wasn't convinced, in more recent times, that democracy was a commodity that could be exported.) Personally, I can't think of any war as a 'good war'. But I have had to concede that there have been necessary wars. Though today, as wars rage in too many parts of the world, I feel considerable unease at the flow of arms. Wars, perpetuated by the supply of arms and military aid, take a massive human toll, potentially even on generations yet to be born.

It is to my greatest surprise that I have learnt so much about my father's life since he died. In many ways, it was a case of having no way of knowing what I didn't know. I hope dad's grandchildren, as they grow up, will come to know both sides of the coin – the valour and the horror. Never forgetting the phenomenal sacrifice and courage of those who fought for freedom during the Second World War, or the terrible cost with which it came. If I could go back in time, I would add to the eulogy I gave at my father's funeral. I would pay far greater tribute to the unremitting bravery he demonstrated as an air gunner during the war. I would humbly thank him for the part he played in preserving freedom. Of course you only get one shot at a eulogy and I'm sure my father would have been happy with the eulogy my sister and I gave at his funeral: a memorable funeral for a resilient man who, truth be told, must just have been grateful to live until nearly 90 against such incredible odds.

After dad's funeral, we were all standing around drinking cups of tea. Everyone seemed to have learnt something new about him during the speeches. One after the other, friends and family members I spoke to said what a lovely funeral it was, and how they'd had no idea about certain aspects of my father's multi-faceted life. It speaks to the private, introspective person that he was. I was about to learn something new that day too. One of dad's friends, who I had never met before, said to me as we chatted, 'Ian was very pleased that he never killed anyone during the war.' Not knowing nearly so much about his war experiences at the time, I was staggered to hear this. I'd just assumed when you went to war as an air gunner, well, you killed people. I couldn't help but feel relieved to learn my father hadn't directly killed anyone. I guess it's a moot point. When you're part of a bomber crew with a mission to drop bombs, there may well be lives lost. Somehow though, rightly or wrongly, learning my father hadn't directly killed anyone by the work of his own hands, was a piece of the jigsaw that sat well with me.

My father was often quiet and detached, so it wasn't until he was gone that I grasped the scale of his presence in my life or the depth of his influence. How fortunate I was to be blessed with someone who was at once a mentor, a role model, a spiritual guide, an intellectual, and a loving father. Uncovering my father's story was a profoundly therapeutic experience, one that provided many unexpected revelations along the way. A lot of things make more sense to me now. In knowing my father better, I know myself better. When someone asked me how retracing my father's time at war had changed me, I thought hard. But then I realised the answer was really quite simple.

'I've become more like my father,' I said.

The preservation of freedom and democracy has become something I have come to care deeply about. Back in 1939 when dad volunteered for war – freedom, democracy, and sovereignty were at stake. I have to confess they weren't things I had spent a great deal of time thinking about until more recently. Perhaps I had taken my freedom and democratic rights for granted. But once I started thinking about them, and the staggering cost at which they had been preserved, I began to hear the words surprisingly often – 'democracy', 'freedom', 'liberty', 'sovereignty'– words still regularly mentioned by politicians, journalists and others. Were they still somewhat elusive goals after all this time, or perhaps ideals that would always be imperfect? With globalisation and the digital revolution creating so much change in the early twenty-first century, the preservation of freedom is as important and relevant as ever. That my father was prepared to die for the cause of freedom makes it hugely significant to me. I can't support the idea of restricting our freedoms for supposed greater security. None of our freedoms and rights came without people dying that we may have them. Today, as we grapple with the challenge of overreaching surveillance, it is critical that government surveillance programmes and businesses operating surveillance based business models do so in ways that protect rather than erode freedom. We must not be the generation who relinquish the courageous work of those who came before us. Transparency and accountability from those with the privilege of power is paramount. The Second World War revealed the worst of what is possible when power is abused. Lest we forget.

Chapter 19

'Slept like tops'

The names of those who in their lives fought for life
Who wore at their hearts the fire's centre.
Born of the sun they travelled a short while towards the sun,
And left the vivid air signed with their honour.

Stephen Spender
New Collected Poems © 2004

War leaves an invisible imprint. If there was one legacy of war that stood out from all the others towards the end of my father's life, it was gratitude: gratitude to have lived a long life, gratitude to God, gratitude to my mother – whose undying love and kindness had helped him through the long nights to find his own inner strength and wisdom, and gratitude to the nuns who had cared for him in Leuven when he lay immobile, an enemy in a foreign land. Privately, he had always dreamed of returning to Leuven to express his gratitude to the nuns. After all, these were the women who had surreptitiously arranged for his 'I'm still alive' letter to be sent to his parents. They were the women who had given him books, chocolates and kindness when he had nothing except the torn clothes on his back. But after the war, dad was no longer much of a traveller. Long haul air travel held little appeal for him. It wasn't until he was invited to attend the Battle of Britain commemoration events in the year 2000, that he was finally persuaded to return to continental Europe. My husband and I seized the opportunity to take my parents on a whistle-stop tour of the continent before the anniversary commemorations began. Knowing it had been many decades since dad had been to Europe (and it hadn't exactly been a holiday the last time), I asked him if there was anywhere in particular he'd like to go.

'Leuven,' he replied without hesitating. With eyes shining at the prospect he added, 'I've always wanted to go back and thank the Sisters who cared for me so well during the war.'

First, we needed to find out if the hospital in Leuven was still in existence. Mrs Troop, at the Belgium Embassy in London, gave us the name and address of Heilig Hart where she felt sure he must have been. We duly navigated our sizeable campervan through Belgium, to the narrow cobblestone streets of central Leuven. I remember remarking how different Europe must look to dad almost sixty years since his last visit. No Nazis to be seen anymore for one, we had said, smiling. Then there was a brief, comfortable silence, anticipation and excitement building as we neared the hospital.

After finding a suitable spot to park the campervan, we headed into the hospital grounds from Hendrik Consciencestraat. As we walked towards the six-story hospital building, everything went into slow motion for me. It was the strangest feeling to know that, at 21 years old, my father had been a patient in this very hospital during the Second World War. I glanced at dad and there were signs of amazed recognition on his face as he took in the hospital and surrounding buildings. I felt as though I was in a documentary to retrace my father's footsteps. We were simultaneously in 1941 and 2000 as we began our pilgrimage to Heilig Hart.

A member of staff directed us to the residence of the Saint Franciscan Sisters of the Sacred Heart. We rang the doorbell and waited, not knowing quite what to expect. My father's reunion with the Sisters is best described in his words. Fortunately his habit of writing a diary while travelling had lived on and this is his excerpt from that day.

Monday 14 August 2000 – We were invited in to where the nuns and sisters lived and prayed. We were received graciously and with great warmth by Sister Chris and another Sister. They listened to my story with great interest and it was soon evident this was indeed the original place. I recognised some details.

They confirmed that it was used in 1941 as a hospital. There was even a 92-year-old Sister who had worked there in 1941 who they brought out to meet us. A dear soul, somewhat frail but still alert. Her memory was vague. They were absolutely delighted that we had called. Plied us with soft drinks and chocolates and biscuits. Gave us some photos of the hospital as it was in 1941. We took photographs and exchanged names and kissed them on both cheeks. Sister Chris had recently acquired facilities for email and we promised to send them photos.

I felt a little emotional to be back there and was really pleased to thank them personally for the kind way they had cared for me so long ago. We left them then as they had prayers to attend. A wonderful atmosphere. We all felt it was a privilege to be allowed into their precincts. All this after fifty-nine years, thanks to Angela and Kannan. It is remarkable how we were guided to find the place all along the way. Leuven is a lovely place, old world with wonderful buildings. We stayed the night in an off road caravan camp, quiet and peaceful and all slept like tops.

It was clear my father had fulfilled a lifelong wish in going back to Leuven. The sincere and profound gratitude he expressed to the Sisters was extraordinary to witness. It was obviously something he had felt compelled to do. Their kindness had touched him deeply and I could see he would rest easier having had the opportunity to express his heartfelt thanks for their extraordinary care all those years ago, when life had otherwise been so bleak.

I learnt something about gratitude that day. I carried it with me when I returned to the Dawn Parade recently, all grown up. It was a very different experience to the Dawn Parade I attended as a little girl. There was of course no newspaper photographer to capture my innocence this time. Nor was I any longer that naïve girl with a poppy. As I paused to remember the fallen, it was with profound respect, gratitude, and humility. I thought especially of Robby, Les, Mac and Pat – extraordinarily brave men who will always live in my heart – and sent them a silent nod of thanks. It was more than seventy years to the day since my father had gone on his first night raid to Nazi Germany. He had fought with the same unconquerable spirit as the Anzac forefathers who had inspired him. I felt profoundly grateful to my father and his fellow servicemen.

My greatest generation father, in life and in death, has had much to teach me. At the end of this journey, having assembled the jigsaw, I have discovered that, when war broke out, he met the challenge with courage and tenacity, and taught me everything I need to know about resilience, gratitude and surrender to a fate beyond one's control. Long may we remember the men who 'left the vivid air signed with their honour,' and salute those who 'in their lives fought for life,' and continue to say for a thousand years, '*This* was their finest hour.'

Yet it is not enough to simply remember. We, the generations that follow, are left to take on the mantle of preserving freedom and democracy. I hope, with all my idealistic heart, the lessons of the past will guide us to a peaceful tomorrow.

Acknowledgements

This book would not have been written without the belief and support of my husband and son, Kannan and Sachin. Grateful thanks to all my friends and family, especially Robyn Walker, Paul Kettel, Mary & Roy Cutler, Susan Bannister, Kate Trevor-Barnston, Laurel Soedjasa, Heather Ogden-Handa, and Michael Zahn. I would like to sincerely thank Ali Orman, Joan Rosier-Jones, the New Zealand Society of Authors, NSW Writer's Centre, Wilhelm Helbig at Kloster Haina, Warrant Officer Roberts at the RAF Marham Heritage Centre, Dave Brocklehurst at the Kent Battle of Britain Museum, Maria Mena at the Arxiu Fotogràfic de Barcelona, John Barjarow, Gayle Cotter for providing information about her Uncle Ivan Robinson, Shirley Yardley for sharing her father Tom Wood's letters from Stalag IX A/H, Jude Boutle for sharing her father's collection of notes and letters, and Andre Bruyninckx of Glabbeek. Thank you to Amber and my book club for your insights and inspiration. Finally, my grateful thanks to Laura Hirst, Karyn Burnham and all the team at Pen & Sword Books.